IS THAT YOU GOD?

God is always speaking to us...
but are we listening?

MIKE McGEOY

Cover and Interior design by KUHN Design Group | kuhndesigngroup.com

Is That You God?
Copyright © 2023 by Mike McGeoy

ISBN 979-8-9892815-0-3 (Paperback)
ISBN 979-8-9892815-1-0 (Ebook)

First paperback edition December 2023

For permission requests contact, mike.mcgeoy@gmail.com

CONTENTS

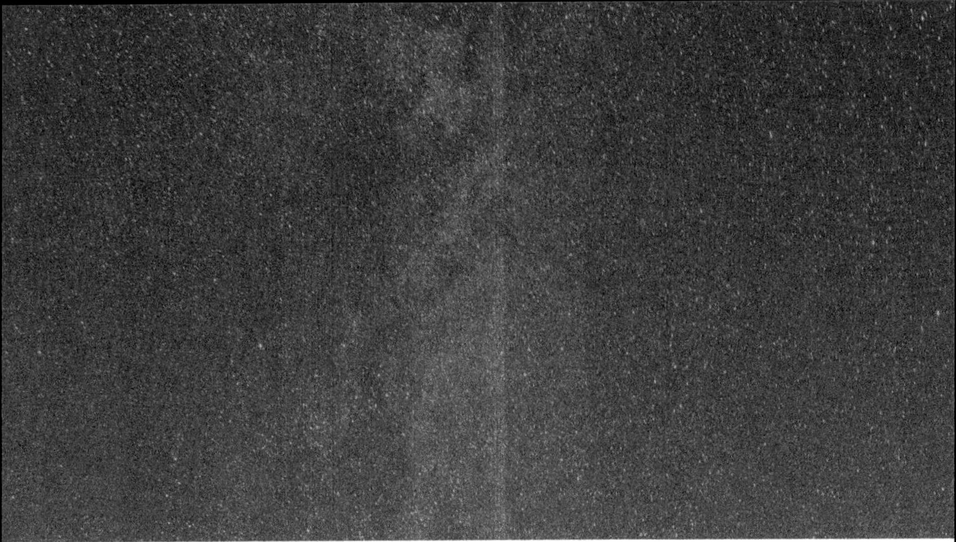

²⁷"My sheep listen to my voice; I know them, and they follow me. ²⁸ I give them eternal life, and they shall never perish; no one will snatch them out of my hand. ²⁹ My Father, who has given them to me, is greater than all; no one can snatch them out of my Father's hand. ³⁰ I and the Father are one." (JOHN 10:27-30, NIV)

INTRODUCTION

y original vision for this book was to build an irrefutable case that humans can hear God's voice. I envisioned a framework that systematically laid out the different ways in which He speaks. It would be sprinkled with a few stories from my personal experiences and would include pertinent verses from the Bible. To give it credibility, I thought I would interview others about their experiences; I didn't want it to just be me talking. With my outline on paper and a rough table of contents in my mind, I was ready to begin the journey. As I wrote and the chapters took shape, I soon realized I had plenty to share from my personal experiences alone. Including others' experiences of hearing God speak could be helpful, but might disrupt the flow of the book. In the end, then, *Is That You God?* is just me telling my unique story about how we can hear God's voice in our lives.

It is a journey that begins at a Christian youth camp in Chile and closes at an independent nondenominational church in Silicon Valley. Along the way, there are signs, dreams, disappointments, and a whole lot of patience on the part of God. My experiences may or may not be distinctive—and they certainly do not make me superior—but they have taught me some lessons that I would like to share with you.

At the risk of giving away the ending, here is what my personal experiences have taught me: *If we are listening, we can hear His voice pretty much everywhere!*

We can hear His voice in nature, like in the pounding of waves on the rocks at our favorite beach.

We can hear His voice through others. This is true in chance meetings with someone new, and in daily interactions with people we already know.

We can hear His voice in the experiences, both sensational and mundane, that happen over the course of our lives, like the miraculous birth of a child or the healing of a dear friend stricken with cancer. Our dreams are also another vehicle that God uses to reveal His voice to us. But we must be cautious of some dreams, especially nightmares, as they can be used by God's adversary.

We can certainly hear God's voice when we read the Bible or listen to an inspirational sermon in church. But if we are paying attention, God's voice can also be heard when the message is not inspirational!

His voice often fills the lyrics of a song and the harmonies and melodies that accompany them. This is not only true for "church" music. I believe with all my heart that God's Spotify or Pandora playlists have just as much Led Zeppelin, Beatles, and Taylor Swift as they do gospel music!

Sometimes we hear God's voice when we commune with Him through prayer, although most of the time we are too busy asking for things to hear what He might be saying. When we treat Him as a cosmic

Santa Claus, we probably are not open to what He wants to tell us. And sometimes what He wants to tell us is an emphatic No!

We also hear His voice in books, magazines, movies, social media, and many other forums. I have heard His voice in all these places, but we must be aware that the media is exploitable as well.

In short, my life has taught me to listen for God—and then to try to listen to God. I wish I had done both earlier and more often in my life. But I know in my heart that God has been with me all along.

And with that, I invite you to join me on this journey of sharing my experiences of hearing God's voice. Who knows? Maybe you will hear God's voice somewhere in this book. I certainly hope you do!

CHAPTER 1

ANOTHER RESTLESS NIGHT

[4]"Early in the morning, Jesus stood on the shore, but the disciples did not realize that it was Jesus.

[5]He called out to them, "Friends, haven't you any fish?"

"No," they answered.

He said, "Throw your net on the right side of the boat and you will find some." When they did, they were unable to haul the net in because of the large number of fish.

Then the disciple whom Jesus loved said to Peter, "It is the Lord!" As soon as Simon Peter heard him say, "It is the Lord," he wrapped his outer garment around him (for he had taken it off) and jumped into the water." (JOHN 21:5-7 NIV)

My hyperactive mind prevents me from sleeping well on most nights. This is not my choice; it's just the way God designed me. I don't actually have trouble falling asleep, as many people do. My problem is an overactive brain. As my wife will attest, most nights I doze off within minutes of my head hitting the pillow. Once into a deep sleep, though, my brain replays the events of the day or launches into an analysis of some troubling issue from work.

No matter how hard I try, my brain will not stop spinning. In this state of semi-slumber, I have resolved some of the world's most difficult challenges with great clarity. If only I could record my stream of consciousness on these nights, I might be in the running for the Nobel Peace Prize! Of course, when morning finally rolls around, I've forgotten most of the brilliant ideas that came to me. It's as if that part of the brain needs to take the daytime hours off.

What I do remember, however, is what time I wake up from my dreams. Besides having an overactive brain, I also have this uncanny ability to know, almost to the minute, what time it is. I'm especially good at night.

I first learned of my time-telling superpower in the seventh grade, when my friend Ephraim was spending the night. We conversed from different sides of the dark room for hours. Barely able to keep my eyes open, I asked him what time it was. Ephraim was one of the few kids in our seventh-grade class who wore a watch. It was this cool "diver's watch" that glowed in the dark and was waterproof in depths of up to sixty meters, where I guess it must be really dark. Instead of telling me the time, Ephraim raised his arm in the air and asked, "What time do you think it is?"

"Midnight!" I replied. After a flip of his wrist to check, Ephraim flew out of bed and bounded across the room with his glowing wrist leading the way. Sure enough, his watch read exactly 12:00 a.m.!

Isn't it funny the things we remember? Sometimes we remember things with such clarity we get a complete mental picture, almost like we are experiencing it again. Unlike déjà vu, this is not just a *feeling* of having been there before. We *know* we have been there before. My experience with Ephraim was so memorable that the picture became burned into my brain. Putting on my amateur psychologist hat, my explanation for the reason people remember seemingly trivial events like this so well is that they sense a unique ability is being revealed in the process. As far as I knew, having a fine-tuned inner-body clock was something nobody else possessed. For a kid who had spent a good part of his early life wondering if he mattered, having a unique talent was something to hang on to.

To this day, I like to play a game with myself in the middle of the night to hone my time-guessing talent. The clock on my wife's nightstand is turned to one side to shield us from its bright green numbers. To play the game, I must get up on my elbow and lean over her sleeping body to see what time it is. The game is simple. Before rolling over,

I guess the time in my head. Invariably, I am never more than three or four minutes off. I can't even count the number of times I have hit it right on the nose, sometimes multiple times during the night. You're probably thinking right now, "What a stupid game!" Truth be told, if I had a choice, I wouldn't play the darn game! I don't really control whether I play the game, though; it just happens. Like I said, my bedtime mind is hyperactive.

What does all of this have to do with listening to God? With that question, I take you to precisely 4:43 a.m., early in the morning of January 22, 2010, when I woke from my usual state of restlessness. I had guessed 4:45 a.m., only two minutes off. My internal clock was ticking as usual. Also, as usual, my restlessness on this night was due to whatever had been running through my mind just before dozing off. Before falling asleep, I had started a brief conversation with God. You might call it a prayer. I apologized that we had not spoken substantively in a while.

Sometimes I'll start praying and then just doze off mid-thought. Do you think God gets a little peeved when I do this? Think about it. Wouldn't you get annoyed if someone you were having a conversation with just closed their eyes and started snoring mid-sentence? Okay, so maybe God doesn't get peeved at us, but I'm pretty sure my waking at 4:43 a.m. was like God nudging my shoulder and saying, "Come on, finish what you were saying. I have something to say to you!"

When I awoke, I had the strongest sense that God was talking to me and had a particular message He wanted me to hear. It was a simple message and one I heard loud and clear: "WRITE THE BOOK!" I had contemplated writing a book for five years but never started it. The message God shared with me that night finally gave me the impetus to stop procrastinating and start writing!

As I lay there, halfway between fully awake and fully asleep, I thought of the times in my life when I had heard the voice of God in clear and unmistakable tones. I am not talking, of course, of sounds that would be audible to anyone outside of my head. Rather, God's voice spoke in words, images, and signs clearly showing to me the author was my Heavenly Father. In my semi-slumber, and in an almost dreamlike state, I went through a mental inventory of at least three or four previous times when my heart had told me in no uncertain terms that God had spoken to me. What struck me was that, while these events stood out in my mind as sensational, there had also been times where I heard God's voice under more mundane circumstances.

I believe what God was telling me at 4:43 a.m. was to *stop putting off this book!* What I have yet to determine is whether the message was sensational or mundane!

And so, filled with the belief that God had given me an unambiguous command, I arose from my bed, quietly got dressed, kissed my wife gently on the head, and headed out. My target on this dark and chilly morning was the Starbucks I passed every morning on my way to work. The journey had begun!

For the next year and a half or so, I got up every Friday morning around 5:30 a.m. and headed to the same Starbucks, laptop in tow, and just wrote. Momentum was hard to maintain at first. There were some days where I wrote very little, but I kept plugging away.

I had heard God's voice that night. He had said to me in no uncertain terms, "WRITE THE BOOK!" So, that is what I did.

CHAPTER 2

WE HEAR, BUT ARE WE LISTENING?

[7] Now Samuel did not yet know the Lord: The word of the Lord had not yet been revealed to him.

[8] A third time the Lord called, "Samuel!" And Samuel got up and went to Eli and said, "Here I am; you called me."

Then Eli realized that the Lord was calling the boy. [9] So Eli told Samuel, "Go and lie down, and if he calls you, say, 'Speak, Lord, for your servant is listening.'" So Samuel went and lay down in his place.

The Lord came and stood there, calling as at the other times, "Samuel! Samuel!"

Then Samuel said, "Speak, for your servant is listening." (1 SAMUEL 3:7-10 NIV)

ave you ever heard someone say, "That was a God moment"? It's usually uttered with the same excitement and gestures that we might use when describing an incredible play we saw on ESPN. It's also often reserved for conversations between two or more church folks. Exclamations attributing something to God don't always receive a universal "Amen!" from fellow believers. And they usually don't fly with most nonbelievers, either.

I must confess, with embarrassment, that I have employed these kinds of expressions on certain occasions, but it felt strange when I did. "It's a God thing" is a way of gaining attention when telling a story. It's like we're saying, "God was involved in this cool thing, but focus on me because God spoke to me!" That's arrogant, don't you think? Why can't we just relate the story and let those who hear it decide whether God was involved?

As you may have guessed, this is the approach I am trying to take in writing to you. I want to recount how I've encountered God in many ways. Then you decide for yourself what to make of me and my story. You might decide that maybe I'm just tooting my horn to get you to think, "What a 'godly' person this guy must be!" Or you might decide that maybe there is something to the notion that God speaks to us on a personal level.

If God does speak to us, then how does He do so? In all humility, here is what I believe: Sometimes God speaks in a gentle whisper, but sometimes He uses a two-by-four upside the head. God's voice is always noticeable through one or more of our senses. And He always communicates in a manner that has a specific significance to the individual in question, even if it sounds strange to others. Sometimes He speaks through His creation, and sometimes through other people. Sometimes He speaks through combinations of words, whether they are on a page or out of someone's mouth. With each passing year, I'm more convinced that God is *always* speaking to us.

Sadly, I have also come to understand that most of the time we aren't open to His attempts to communicate. I know this mostly through my personal experiences. We're often too busy with life's problems. We believe in our ability to solve things through our own efforts and thoughts. It never occurs to us that the solutions that suddenly become clear to us—the inspiration we get from a friend or even the words we read on a billboard—might be the voice of God trying to get our attention.

It's like the joke about the Christian guy who wakes up one morning to find the flood waters surrounding his house. A neighbor drives by in an SUV and offers to drive him to safety. "No thank you," the guy replies. "I am waiting on God to save me." After another hour, the rising waters force him upstairs to the second story, where he looks out to see a neighbor in a rowboat pull up to the window and tell him to get in. Again, the guy waves off a would-be rescuer, saying,

"I am waiting on God to bring me to safety." Finally forced to climb onto the roof of his home, the man politely waves off the offer of a rope dangling from a police helicopter. "No thanks. I'm waiting on God!" Within minutes of this third offer, the man is swept off the roof by the raging current and drowns. As he is walking through the pearly gates, he spots God and approaches Him to ask, "God, why did you let me drown? I'm confused. Haven't I been a faithful servant to you all these years? I prayed you would rescue me repeatedly, but you never showed up!"

God gently replies, "I sent an SUV, a rowboat, and a helicopter—what more did you want me to do?"

The man, like many Christians, was resolute in his prayers but neglected to notice God's response to them.

I believe that God has never stopped talking to us, whether through dramatic means or relatively conventional ones. I make this point because some theologians suggest that God stopped talking directly to His people after the Old Testament times. In other words, burning bushes, talking donkeys, and booming voices from Mount Sinai are things of the past. Now, this book isn't about the theology of hearing God's voice. It is not an attempt to convince you with textual evidence from Scripture or scientifically verifiable proof that, yes, God still talks to His people. Again, I can only attest to my experiences. And they tell me that God is still speaking.

The problem is that we often are not able to listen. As we have become more and more inundated with technologies that allow us to stay connected all day, every day, we have drowned out His voice. It's not that God cannot use those vehicles to communicate with us, but let's be honest: when we constantly scan our Twitter or Instagram feeds, or endlessly scroll through Facebook, it is generally for entertainment purposes. We aren't going there in the hopes that God will speak to us. Even if God did choose to use social media to try to reach us, picking out his voice from all the noise, rhetoric, and media sound bites would be next to impossible!

For the sake of argument and regardless of your personal beliefs, let's just assume that my argument that God still communicates with His followers is correct. The question then becomes, how do we hear His voice? My humble opinion is that it starts with something simple. It starts with the simple belief that God does talk to us. It continues with the courage and faith to attribute to God those things that we see in our lives that we cannot explain. And it helps greatly if, when we get those inklings, we can just stand back for a moment and say, "Wow, that was cool!"

My conviction has grown that God talks to us daily. He communicates with us in a manner that is both calculated and unique, reaching us wherever we are. The sad reality, however, is that the conversation is mostly one-sided. I say this not to suggest that God is domineering or uninterested in what we have to say. I believe He is supremely interested in us. All of us. Every man, woman, and child on earth. This includes individuals who don't share my belief in God or any God. Whether we use the label Christian, Jewish, Muslim, Buddhist, Shaker, Quaker, Unitarian, Catholic, Methodist, nondenominational, multidenominational, conservative, fundamentalist, New Age, Wiccan, emergent, convergent, agnostic, or even atheist to describe our faith, God is interested in us all. But we often ignore Him due to the noise in our busy lives.

Since the beginning, God has communicated with us personally. Through the beauty and splendor of His creation, through the thousands of people that we cross paths within our lives, and through the collective experiences of our lifetimes, He is speaking with us. But we often aren't listening!

CHAPTER 3

I KNOW THAT HE IS NOT!

[12]"I have much more to say to you, more than you can now bear. [13] But when he, the Spirit of truth, comes, he will guide you into all the truth. He will not speak on his own; he will speak only what he hears, and he will tell you what is yet to come. [14] He will glorify me because it is from me that he will receive what he will make known to you." (JOHN 16:12-14 NIV)

cannot claim to have ever heard the voice of God externally. But I have heard God's voice clearly. I have heard no tone, no pitch, no accent, no cadence, and no rhythm—none of the things that one might attribute to an audible sound. But there have been moments when the words that came to my mind were as understandable as if spoken by someone next to me.

Some years back, when I was out of work and surfing Internet job boards, the doorbell rang one morning. Anxious for a break from the drudgery of job searching, I dashed down the stairs to the front door. There before me stood two all-American young men who wore the pressed black pants, white-collared shirt, black tie, and nametag that Mormon Church missionaries have made famous around the world. Ordinarily, I would have greeted this class of visitor with a benign brush-off: "Thanks, but I have a church, and I'm quite content there—good luck and have a great day!"

But that day, I checked my cynicism and engaged them. Maybe I was just bored, or perhaps my innate curiosity with the Mormon Church was surfacing. I've had many friends over the years who were Mormons.

One of our neighbors, an ex-NFL player, was a devout Mormon whom I liked and respected immensely. One year at Christmas, he invited my son and me to attend a special service at the Mormon Temple in Oakland, California, where we got to hear and see some San Francisco 49ers players. Part of the evening included a self-guided tour through one of the temple buildings, which felt more like a museum than a church. There were full-sized wax figures positioned in beautifully constructed scenes, much like one would see in a large metropolitan museum. As we wound through the carefully designed tour, we saw scenes that looked to be right out of the Bible. We saw the figure of Jesus holding a child on His lap while speaking to a group of men, likely the apostles. Next, we saw Jesus standing in front of a gathering of locals, their faces fixed on him, listening intently to His words. And then we came upon Jesus standing at the side of a river talking with Native Americans. *"What?"* I thought. *"What?"* Although I still don't read the Bible as much as I should, I have never seen any references to Native Americans. Visiting the temple was different from what I was expecting, but we did get to see the NFL Hall of Famer Steve Young!

Anyway, these two young men seemed to be friendly and well-intentioned, so I welcomed them in. The Mormon Church is officially called "The Church of Jesus Christ of Latter-Day Saints," I reasoned. Besides, who was I to judge? They were just as sure of their faith as I was, and they were willing to walk door to door to share it with other people. Listening to what they had to say seemed like the Christian thing to do.

I listened politely to the two young men for ten minutes, resisting the urge to interject, when I heard something that went against what my faith had taught me. I told them I appreciated their taking the time to meet with me. I added that, while there were some things they had explained to me that seemed rational, I had a problem with some of the foundational tenets of the Mormon faith.

Not to be deterred, one of the young evangelists handed me a crisp new copy of the Book of Mormon and issued the following challenge: "Start with pages one through three in the Introduction, then read the first chapter of Nephi, and then pray to God and ask Him two questions: *Is this book the word of God? and Is Joseph Smith a prophet of God?*"

Before leaving, they asked when they could return. Being that I was unemployed at the time, with no job prospects on the horizon, I told them to stop by around the same day and time next week.

With a resolve to make an honest attempt at keeping my end of the bargain, I retreated to what my wife sometimes called "the cave," the spare room we had built over the garage that housed our family's personal computer. With my head bowed, I said a quick prayer, asking God to give me an open mind, and then I opened the book. Uncharacteristically, in light of my usual cynicism, I found myself engaged in the introduction as I read it slowly. What I was reading appeared to be plausible!

Next was the Book of Nephi. Reading with an open mind, I thought, "This sounds like the Bible … "

With my assignment complete, it was now time to put the matter before God in prayer. Rising from the chair, I kneeled and closed my eyes. I took a second to clear my mind and then began the first of the two prayers that the young Mormons had urged me to pray: "Father, is this book from you?"

Almost immediately, these exact words rang in my head: "I know that it is not!"

I followed with: "Father, is Joseph Smith one of your prophets?"

And with the same lightning speed and unmistakable clarity of the first response, I heard these words: "I know that he is not."

Smiling, I repeated the words, "I know that he is not."

And with that, I knew God had spoken. If the room had been full of people, no one else would have heard the words. But I received them with such strength and clarity that there was no room for ambiguity in my mind regarding who they came from and what they meant! "I know that he is not!" Who the heck speaks like that, anyway? Had I been the one speaking, the words would have been a simple, "No way, dude!"

I spent the rest of the week in eager anticipation of the return of the Mormon missionaries. When the doorbell rang on that morning, I said a quick prayer for strength and courage and then bounded down the stairs with the anticipation of a five-year-old on Christmas morning. I greeted the two young men and cheerfully thanked them for coming back. Standing before them, I waited eagerly for them to ask if I had done the reading and said the prayer.

I honestly do not remember if they ever got the chance to talk, or if I just jumped right in. Either way, after I recounted my experience about the reading, my prayer, and the response from God, it was like the air had been sucked out of the room. My response was not what they had been looking for. Eventually, the bolder of the two, with a look of bewilderment that said, "They didn't teach us how to respond to this," asked if they could show me a videotape, they had brought with them. I politely declined. They seemed like nice fellows, but I already had God's word on the matter.

CHAPTER 4

SISTER MARY FRANK

²¹ "Whether you turn to the right or to the left, your ears will hear a voice behind you, saying, "This is the way; walk in it."
(ISAIAH 30:21 NIV)

A s is true of many folks in the United States, my initial religious upbringing differed significantly from my current one. Today, I would consider myself a nondenominational Protestant, or simply a follower of Jesus Christ. As the product of an Irish Catholic father and a Methodist mother, however, I was raised in my father's tradition.

In that day and age, there were three effective laws in the Catholic Church. First, you baptized your children as infants. Second, you sent your kids to parochial schools. And third, while not technically required, you named your first son Michael. While neither of my parents were devout in their religion, they saw the value of following those laws! Hence, three siblings and I were baptized as infants and attended parochial schools, at least initially. Finally, as you hopefully gathered by looking at the cover of the book, my given name is Michael. In my second-grade class of maybe twelve or thirteen boys, no fewer than eight of us shared the name Michael!

The sisters (or nuns) never called us by our first names, though; they just called us Mr. McGeoy, Mr. Flynn, and so on. One day, a bunch of us Michaels were out on the front lawn of the school enjoying the first snow of winter when one of the nuns came out the main door and told us to stop throwing snowballs lest someone get hurt. "Yes, Sister Mary Frank," we all chimed in unison as we quickly dropped the evidence in our hands. I always thought it funny that the nuns all had two names: one male and one female and always preceded by "Sister."

After waiting a couple of minutes to ensure the sister wasn't watching, we casually started tossing small handfuls of snow at each other, making sure not to draw too much attention. Within no time, we were back to packing fluffy snowballs and working out our arms. Bending over to make a tight little snowball, I had visions of throwing a perfect strike at one of the other Mikes, who was maybe twenty-five feet from me. As I wheeled around to send the icy missile towards him, Sister Mary Frank, who had been watching from a window, stepped right in front of my target. I watched in terror as my perfectly thrown snowball hit the nun square in the chest and exploded with a thud. Within a flash, I was being dragged by the ear into the Mother Superior's office, where I sat alone for what seemed like an eternity. I never actually got in trouble that day, as neither Sister Mary Frank nor the Mother Superior returned to the office. Years later, as I look back on that day, my guess is that they knew that sitting alone in the waiting room and wondering what was in store for me was punishment enough!

And then there was the time I forgot my lunch and, along with a girl in my class, was told to report to Sister Beatrice Joseph at the rectory. We knocked meekly on the large wooden door, and an older nun met us. She asked why we were there, and I choked out a teary-eyed, "We forgot our lunches." Sister Beatrice Joseph told us sternly (or at least that is how I remember it) to sit down on the steps, and then she closed the door with punctuation. Believing that we had both committed a sin, we huddled together for what seemed like forever, tears streaming down our cheeks. When the door opened again, we saw the rosy smile of Sister Beatrice Joseph, who was carrying a tray of hot food meant just for us. Thanking the sister, we devoured our bounty and then rushed off to join our friends for the last few minutes of recess, vowing that neither of us would ever forget our lunch again! While many who have experienced the Catholic school route say that the use of shame and guilt scarred them for life, I look back on those days with some fondness, although that nine-year-old little boy inside me probably is not as forgiving.

Catholic school was my first glimpse inside religion, the Church, and I guess God, ultimately. Thinking back on those years, I don't remember God, or Jesus, being a big part of the equation in my early life. The Church often presented God as someone to fear, despite portraying Him as a loving figure. But this was not fear in the sense of reverence or respect. It was the kind of fear that said, if you step out of line, He is waiting to zap you from the cosmos. Even First Communion, which is supposed to be a joyous rite of passage in a young Catholic's life, was marred by being made to feel guilt and shame. Practicing for First Communion one day at the church of our school (Holy Redeemer in Kensington, Maryland), I threw up into the pew in front of me and all over the crimson carpet that served as a path to the altar. Maybe there was a flu bug going around because, at almost the same time, a little girl in my class threw up as well. We were both briskly whisked away into one of the many side chambers of the church and, while the sister cleaned up our vomit, we were made to feel guilty for the big mess we had made in the church! How dare we desecrate the church like that!

I share these stories with you not to disparage the Catholic Church but simply to show that, like most people, my earliest experiences with religion comprise many things, both good and bad. And ALL of them played a part in how I came to view who God is. One attribute that I think is best illustrated in these short stories is that God has a great sense of humor! In fact, I think that humor is, yet another way God speaks to us.

CHAPTER 5

DO YOU SEE WHAT I SEE?

[1]"In the past, God spoke to our ancestors through the prophets at many times and in various ways, [2]but in these last days he has spoken to us by his Son, whom he appointed heir of all things, and through whom also he made the universe." (HEBREWS 1:1-2 NIV)

During the summer of 1975, when I was sixteen years old, I had a conversion experience at a youth retreat south of Santiago, Chile. The first time in my life that I really heard God. Back in the first chapter of the book, I mentioned my belief that God has spoken to me in both "sensational" and "mundane" circumstances. When I say mundane, that description relates to the settings in which I found myself, not to the quality of God's voice! In fact, the following story certainly ranks among the most sensational of experiences in my life and undoubtedly set the stage for my spiritual journey and for this book.

How did I end up in a different hemisphere? It all began in the summer of 1969, when my mother came home one day and told us we would move to California to be closer to my father, who was in the Navy. After returning from a sixteen-month stint in Vietnam, he had been stationed at the Oak Knoll Naval Hospital in Oakland. My mother had flown out there in the early spring to meet him, and I am sure that he talked her into making the move. I was extremely excited to be closer to him, but I'm not sure what was in it for mom. She and my father were divorced by then, and her family all lived close to us in Maryland. I suppose a change of scenery and a chance to start a new life were motivators for her, as was her children's happiness.

Not knowing anything about California, I didn't realize at first that Ventura, where we would end up living, was almost four hundred miles away from Oakland. Well, I then thought, at least we would be on the same side of the country! As it happened, none of that would matter. Not more than a couple of weeks after we settled into our new house, a man whom my mother had dated for a short while before we moved showed up one day and proposed to her. She said yes, and before we knew it, we headed back east, to Washington, DC. Within two months, we were on a plane to Tel Aviv, Israel, where I would live for the next four years. While it was hard being pulled away from my father yet again and leaving family and friends in Maryland, my years in Israel were some of the best years of my life.

Israel is such a beautiful country with so much history, and even though there was a constant threat of war and terrorism, my friends and I had the kind of freedom to roam around and explore that parents today would never afford their kids. My cherished memories include riding horseback through sand dunes that engulfed ancient Roman aqueducts, haggling with Arab merchants in the old city of Jerusalem, and running on the very beaches that Jesus walked with his disciples!

These were also some of the least spiritual years of life, unfortunately. From the end of my illustrious parochial school career to this point, I do not recall ever setting foot inside any kind of church. I remember going to a Baptist missionary camp every summer in Israel, but the camp did not include any semblance of a church that I can remember. Yet God was getting ready to speak to me.

Fast-forward a few years, and I was now a high school student at an international school in Santiago, Chile. Early in my sophomore year, I fell for an attractive girl in the class named Jennifer. She was a "born-again" Christian. Despite having no clue exactly what that meant, and not really caring anyway, I suddenly found myself a regular church attendee for the first time in my young life. Truth be told, I attended mostly out of a desire to spend as much time as possible with my girlfriend. But, as I have come to understand, God can take whatever we give Him!

Skip ahead two years to the first week back at school after summer vacation. My friends and I were looking forward to our senior year and all the good times in store for us. The school had scheduled a "Welcome Back to School" dance, which I was eagerly looking forward to. Then I got word from Jennifer that she would not be going, because she had committed, along with some of the other girls in the church senior high youth group, to be a chaperone at a weekend youth retreat for our church. While I actually did not mind all that much that she would miss the dance, I was sure to let her know that, although it just wouldn't be the same without her, I would try to somehow have a good time in her absence. Then my free weekend vanished before my eyes when she informed me they were short on male chaperones and that I should come along to help. Talk about a reversal of fortunes. I was planning a weekend with just my buddies, and suddenly I was drafted to chaperone eight- and nine-year-old boys at a church retreat!

After a little more conversation and coaxing by Jennifer, I "happily" agreed to go along. Jennifer had suggested that it would be okay for me to bring along a friend. Like my attendance at the retreat, the response to this suggestion was preordained, as her best friend Sandy, who was also going to the retreat, had a thing for a friend of mine named Peter. It didn't matter that Peter was Catholic and that the church the rest of us attended was not. I was pretty sure that he would go along just to make the Sandy connection. So now, Peter and I were off to our first church retreat! The weekend started off with the requisite bus trip to the retreat site, which was tucked away in the idyllic foothills of the Andes Mountains, a little more than one hour from the church. Packed full of sleeping bags, noisy kids, and a handful of slightly reluctant teenagers, the bus set off for our destination, ringing with the sounds of children singing church songs. I'm pretty sure that we didn't sing "Ninety-nine Bottles of Beer on the Wall," but a few of us would not have minded passing the time that way.

Upon arrival at the retreat site, we looked out at a breathtaking view of the property. I'm not sure if the Garden of Eden had a large log cabin lodge in the center, but if it did, then it was surely like the one at the retreat. The dirt road off the main highway rose to an elevation of maybe two or three hundred feet and came to rest in front of the main lodge, which was surrounded by luscious lawns, terraced gardens, and large eucalyptus trees that dwarfed everything around them.

As we unpacked the bus, Jill, the pastor's wife, informed us that the girls would sleep in the lodge and the boys would stay in tents in one of the garden areas down the hill, maybe one hundred feet from the lodge. After we all got situated, the rest of the evening passed by with dinner, songs, games, and the admonition to "get a good night's sleep" from Jill, who was leading the retreat.

The next morning, we all met in the lodge for breakfast and some instructions on how the weekend was to unfold. Then the group moved outside to a spacious lawn in front of the lodge for some teaching. To this day, I remember nothing about Jill's original message that morning. But something else happened during the teaching that would change the weekend for many of us and has stuck in my mind to this day.

After maybe forty-five minutes of Jill's teaching, some of the younger kids got antsy and ultimately disruptive, as children who are asked to sit quietly in a circle are bound by the laws of nature to do. As the noise level rose, Jill held up her hand for quiet. Then, with a solemn face, she informed us that "Satan" was in our midst, and that he was trying to disturb our time together. Talk about a group of people going instantly silent! And then, with all the collected tone of someone who delivered this kind of revelation frequently, Jill explained to the group how Satan hated it when people got together to talk about Jesus. She pointed out that by inserting a little noise and chaos into the group, he had stopped the teaching and lessons that centered on Jesus and God. While her admonition caught me off guard, I was inclined to pay even closer attention, as her mentoring had become hugely important in my young life.

Wow, this was all brand new to me! From what I knew, Satan was just some mythical character in the Bible who represented evil. Dressed in red, complete with horns, tail, and a pitchfork, he lived in hell. A quick scan around the circle revealed nobody or nothing that fit that description.

To say that Jill's revelation piqued our curiosity would be an understatement. We fired questions at her, in rapid succession, and would have continued all day had she not stopped us. After fielding a few of our impassioned queries, which came mostly from the older students, Jill told us we could talk more about it later that evening, after the younger kids had gone to bed. The rest of the day was a blur as we eagerly anticipated learning more about this "Satan" guy.

When dinner was over and the younger kids had settled in for the night, the group of high school students and Jill moved into a quiet room in the lodge to resume our talk about Satan. With most of that day to mull over what she had told us, the questions again flooded out. For the next two hours, we listened to Jill expound upon the persona of Satan. We learned and talked about who he was, and how he came to be evil. We learned what his mission was, and what he could and could not do. And mostly we learned how he operated and why we should fear him. By the end of our talk, we all had a genuine and newfound sense and fear of Satan. As the hour was late, Jill closed the session with the loving assurance that, as evil and powerful as Satan was, God had already defeated him through His son, Jesus Christ. Thus, all we needed to do to be safe from Satan was to have Jesus in our hearts.

I can honestly say that I had never been more terrified in my life. I was even more scared than the night when my group of friends and I went downtown to watch a late-night showing of *The Exorcist* in a sleazy run-down theater. Talk about a fun bus ride home! The scene where Regan speaks to the priest in Latin still makes the hair on the back of my neck stand up to this day!

Unsure of what awaited us, Peter and I said good night to Jill and the girls and headed into the frosty night air towards our tent. To say we felt "evil in the air" would be an understatement of the greatest proportions. We peered across the vast lawn down to the gardens below, where our tent was shrouded in a darkness that eclipsed even the surrounding night. I informed Peter that I sensed we were in genuine jeopardy. I felt silly for getting so scared by the stories our youth pastor had told us, yet I could not deny the fear for my life that I felt at that moment.

Motioning to the wooden bench that hugged the wall of the lodge, I whispered to Peter that I wasn't ready to go down to the tent at just that moment. Sitting together on the bench as close as two people could without sitting on each other, Peter and I reviewed what we had just heard. We both agreed it scared us shitless, and that "Satan" was no longer a myth to us. The more we talked about Satan, the more the sense of evil seemed to grow around us.

Looking over at the pastor's car, which was parked under an arbor not ten feet from us, I got the distinct sense that it was possessed by a demon. The small metallic bumper curved up in an evil grin. The car had not been running for at least eight hours, but its headlights had tiny red lights at their centers. The shape and size of the front grill completed the demonic face and sent shivers up my spine. I knew from the Exorcist that Satan possessed little girls, but could he do the same with a car? Wanting to make sure that I wasn't just losing my mind, I pointed to the car and asked Peter if he saw anything. He confirmed my fears by describing precisely what I had seen. How could that be? How could we both be seeing the same thing? I closed my eyes for a few seconds and tried to push the picture out of my mind, hoping that when I opened them, the face would be gone. But it did not go away.

How could any of this be true? Growing up Catholic, I had heard stories about apparitions of the Virgin Mary, but I was always so skeptical. Up to that point in my young life, if someone had told me about some supernatural experience or vision, they had experienced,

I would not have believed them. Yet how could I deny what I was seeing, feeling, and experiencing at this moment?

The banter between Peter and me was constant now. We both were afraid that if we stopped speaking, the darkness that surrounded us might swallow us up. I figured that the best way to get the evil car out of my mind was to turn away and try to focus on something else. Looking out at the night sky, I couldn't help but notice the large row of eucalyptus trees that bordered the property and towered over our campsite below. The wind, which had been motionless moments before, quickly picked up and created a disturbance among the trees. I nudged Peter and motioned in their direction.

Almost as if on cue, the swaying branches and leaves of the mighty trees formed a hideous face, half beast, half man, laughing at us with the same sardonic smile as the haunted automobile. Turning away, I glanced back at the car to see if it had morphed back into its natural state. But no dice. Satan was now indwelling the car and the surrounding trees. As far as we were concerned, we were next.

Drawing closer to Peter, I whispered I was "really" scared; he concurred. Reaching deep into my mind for some form of relief, I recalled the final admonition that Jill had left us with that night: the assurance that, with Jesus' protection, Satan was powerless against us. Trying to remember the exact words of the prayer that she had given us, I leaned into Peter and told him I wanted to ask Jesus into my heart. Would he like too as well? I asked. Without pause, he nodded his assent. After first checking to see if he remembered the substance of the prayer that Jill had given us, I closed my eyes and prayed out loud. I prayed to the Savior of the world that we were sinners, and that we were sorry, and I asked that He please come into our hearts and protect us from Satan.

After maybe thirty seconds of praying out loud, I opened my eyes and glanced at the car to my left. The front of the car still had Satan's smile, but within seconds, the smirk faded from my view. Swinging around, I looked towards the eucalyptus trees to see if Satan had left there as well. His face was still there, taunting me with fiery eyes, the wind seeming to whip his face into an animated frenzy. And then, just as quickly as the winds had come, they stopped. Slowly, the face that only moments before had brought terror into my heart faded, and as it faded, a bright white circle appeared in its place. Evenly spaced around the perimeter of the glowing orb were three small lines or notches.

I searched my mind to make sense of the visual before me. What was the white circle and what did the three lines represent? And then it came to me as clear as day! My Catholic upbringing told me that the glowing white circle, which by now had completely blotted out Satan, represented the wafer or host that the priest raises up as he consecrates it during the communion ceremony. And the three evenly spaced notches on the host immediately signified to me the three persons that make up the "triune" God: the Father, the Son, and the Holy Ghost.

As I had done earlier with the face of Satan on the car and in the trees, I looked away and then back again, hoping that the visions would be gone. But when I looked back into the trees, the "heavenly host" was still there in all its glory. I cannot adequately describe the sense of peace and calm that pervaded my entire mind, body, and soul as we sat almost paralyzed by the spectacle before us.

Again, I checked in with Peter to make sure that I wasn't the only one seeing this miracle of sight unfold. And while I couldn't know for sure if Peter was seeing and experiencing everything exactly as I was, his responses to my questions and promptings showed he too, was indeed experiencing something very profound. The peace and calm that had invaded my being was also washing over Peter. I could see it in his face and hear it in his voice.

While I have since then never felt the level of darkness and fear that I experienced that night, I can vividly recall it to this day. It appeared God had removed the terror and fear that had overwhelmed us just minutes before and replaced it with a feeling of peace and serenity in our souls.

While we knew it was probably time to head down to our tent to get some sleep, we both still had a hint of doubt about what might wait for us in the dark shadows below. The last time we had peered over the stone wall that signaled the descent to the garden, we had seen almost total darkness and felt a foreboding sense of doom. As we approached the path and gazed down toward our tent, what we saw was almost more amazing than the spectacle we had just witnessed in the trees. Our tent was glowing from the inside! It was as if someone had turned on a lantern or a powerful flashlight and then left the tent. The crazy thing was that neither of us had even brought a lantern or a flashlight! As we stood there staring incredulously at the illuminated tent, Peter and I just laughed. With yet another sign before us that Jesus had indeed heard and answered our prayers, we glided down the winding path almost as if walking on air.

Upon entering our tent, we half expected to see a scared young boy holding a flashlight. We both felt a compelling need to check our bags, just to make sure that someone had not been playing a supremely cosmic joke on us. But even as we searched, I knew in my heart that what we had just seen and experienced was not an elaborate hoax. It was not a figment of our collective imagination. How could that have been the case? We had seen the same things! And it certainly was not some hallucinogenic reaction to drugs or rotten food.

My experience remains a clear sign to me that God still communicates with us today. That He speaks to our eyes, our ears, and our hearts in ways that are so personal and so clear that there can be no mistaking who the author is. Of course, we always have the option to discount what we have seen and heard, to chalk it up to coincidence, or to find some other explanation for what has happened. But that was not my experience.

That night, I believed that the creator of the universe had invaded time and space to send me a very clear and personal message—to calm my fears, to give me hope, to speak His love into my heart. While it would be decades before that message would sink in permanently, from that day forward, I knew Jesus had come into my heart and that I had heard from God. As Peter and I slipped into sleep, no doubt exhausted from our emotional experience, I knew that we both had a sense that even if the entire world came crashing down around us, inside of this tent, nothing could harm us.

As we woke up the next morning to the sound of young boys clamoring about in their tents, Peter and I did a quick check-in with each other to make sure that what we had experienced the night before had not been a dream. Still filled with a sense of peace and serenity, we quickly folded up our sleeping bags and bounded out of the tent, eager to share our revelation with the rest of the group.

Honestly, the remainder of the retreat is a blur to me now, as are, to some extent, the days, weeks, and years after that. I know we shared our story with Jill and the others at the retreat and that, at Jill's urging, I shared the story with the entire congregation the following weekend. I still remember the tears in the eyes of so many of the people who sat mesmerized as I shared. And the many people who came to me afterward and thanked me for my testimony. I also remember the whispers and stares from those that doubted my story, those who looked at me as a long-haired teenager who couldn't possibly have experienced God in such a supernatural way. They are people who have gone, or may go, to their graves believing the lie that God stopped talking to His people thousands of years ago.

I chose then to believe, and I've continued to believe with all my heart, that God is talking to us every day. God is talking through the Bible, in the wonders of nature, through other people, through our experiences both good and bad, through music, and even through pain and suffering. The question that I think we need to answer is, once again, are we listening?

CHAPTER 6

BITTERSWEET VALIDATION

² "This is what the Lord says, he who made the earth, the Lord who formed it and established it—the Lord is his name: ³ 'Call to me and I will answer you and tell you great and unsearchable things you do not know.' (JEREMIAH 33: 2-3 NIV)

Replaying that night in my mind over the years, I often wondered if Peter and I had honestly seen the same things. Did he see the pastor's car morph into the face of Satan? Was the hideous face that I saw in the trees the same one that he saw? Did the tent, lit up from inside like a beacon on a hill, appear that way to Peter as well? Or was he just along for the ride? Was he under the "power of suggestion"? In his frightened state, was he open to whatever I offered that night?

Sadly, Peter returned home that weekend to parents who could not, or were unwilling to, believe what their son had to share with them. Some elders in my church could not share in my joy and thus found it easier to brush it off as nonsense, but Peter had to deal with this kind of reaction from his own parents. I recall the sadness on Peter's face the next day at school as he recounted the conversation he had with his parents after returning from the retreat. It no doubt started with all the joy and excitement that Peter had flowing from his heart as a result of his newfound relationship with Jesus and the supernatural events of the weekend. But it ended with the admonition that what he had experienced was "well and good," but that as long as he lived in "this house," he would attend the Catholic Church.

Many years later, I got a call from a friend telling me that Peter was dying. He was in the hospital and likely would not make it. Peter finally succumbed to a long battle with alcoholism, but not before we talked on the phone one last time. Over the years when we had talked, something in his voice, his words, and his demeanor always suggested a life filled with sadness and regret.

To be sure, Peter loved his work and had a wonderful career. Actually, you may have seen him at halftime of the Super Bowl or before the first pitch of a Major League Baseball game. Peter was the guy who released a bald eagle, which then took a majestic flight around the stadium before landing gently on his arm, to thunderous applause. And yet, as cool as Peter's career had been, there was an emptiness in him that is so common in the culture of our day. This emptiness cannot be satisfied by fortune or fame. Too often, it is masked with alcohol, drugs, or any other manner of addictions. Peter had been self-medicating with alcohol for years, and though I had some thoughts about why, I had never gotten the chance to hear from him why his life had become so empty.

After the phone call I knew I needed to speak with Peter. Partly, I wanted to assuage the guilt that comes when one learns that a good friend is struggling. "What could I have done to help him?" I asked myself. Partly, I wanted to get answers to questions about that night together at the youth retreat. But mostly, I wanted to share with him the hope and sense of peace that, so many years after our mutual introduction to the supernatural, I had finally come to experience in my relationship with God . I wanted Peter to know that beyond all the failures in his life, beyond the regrets for choices made or not made, beyond all the pain that had driven him to self-medicate with alcohol, he had a Father in heaven who loved him dearly. He had a Father who would welcome him with open arms when his time, soon as it might be, came.

Having wondered all these years just what Peter remembered of that night, or if indeed he remembered it at all, I wanted to remind him he and I had put our trust in Jesus nearly thirty years ago. I wanted to let him know that the promise God makes to us is that once we ask Him into our hearts, He will come in and never leave us.

When I asked Peter about the youth retreat, he suddenly became animated. In a voice that resounded with life and did not suggest he was a man close to death, he excitedly recounted that night in the garden many years ago. Without prompting, Peter recalled for me his memory of the terror and fear that we had endured after our lesson on Satan. He recounted for me the faces that we had seen, the prayer that we prayed, and the miraculous peace that flowed from it. He shared that he had wondered all these years if I had remembered that night! I had to choke back the tears that were now streaming down my cheek. Tears of joy that came from the confirmation I had just received from my dying friend. Tears of joy that, for all these years, Peter had carried with him the same memories that I had. And tears of joy that, even though sadness and regret had occupied Peter for much of his life, when it was his time to go, he would soon be in the arms of a loving Father.

I thanked God that day for having been able to talk with Peter one more time. To validate the words that God had spoken into our hearts on that dark and eerie night thirty-plus years prior. To share the hope with Peter that even if he lost the battle that he was facing, he had long since won the war. Because he had been willing to open his heart to hear and respond to his Heavenly Father's voice, we would see each other again!

Peter died not long after we talked for the last time. I wasn't there with him during his last days, but I know he went to his grave with a sense of peace much like the one he had experienced—that WE had experienced—as long-haired kids who heard God's voice on a youth retreat south of Santiago, Chile.

CHAPTER 7

WHAT ARE YOU GONNA REMEMBER MORE?

[20]"Here I am! I stand at the door and knock. If anyone hears my voice and opens the door, I will come in and eat with that person, and they with me." (REVELATION 3:20 NIV)

'd love to tell you that in the months and years after my encounter with God at the youth retreat, my life became a continuous series of similar experiences, which then propelled me into a lifelong pursuit of God. But I would be lying if I did! While I continued to attend church (most of the time), my path over the next twenty years would suggest that I was running away from God rather than towards Him. I spent my freshmen year at a "Christian" college in Southern California called Pepperdine. While I attended the required "Intro to the Bible" class and a mandatory school-wide chapel every Wednesday morning, my walk with God was becoming more distant each day. The one thing I held on to was the sense that Jesus would always be in my heart and that He would never desert me.

For financial reasons, I could not return to Pepperdine for my sophomore year, so I continued my education at Santa Barbara City College for one year before transferring to San Jose State University. When asked why I chose San Jose State, my explanation always began with "to be closer to my father"—which seemed like a noble reason. In reality, my second transfer in as many years had much more to do with following my girlfriend up north. As fate would have it, she broke up with me just one week after we got there; she had met someone else right before school started, when I had gone to the beach with my brother and dad for a brief vacation.

But I was in college, and college life meant girls and parties and fraternities... and a few classes here and there. I became famous in my fraternity for a phrase that, to this day, still haunts me. When looking to drag someone along to the campus pub, a midweek party, or even a late-night road trip, I had a standard plea that twisted more than a few arms: "What are you going to remember more: the night you studied for that midterm, or the night you partied with the bros?" It was probably that phrase alone that accounted for me taking seven years to get my diploma.

With so many obligations (or distractions) in college life, there was little time left for going to church and renewing the relationship with God I had begun just a few years before. However, as I would find out more than once in my adult life, even though I put God away in the closet, He wasn't giving up on me. Indeed, considering some of the stupid things I did and choices I made, it is a veritable miracle that I am even alive to be writing this!

Years after college and just a few years into marriage and children, I found myself on a family trip to Disneyland. We drove down there from the Bay Area and, to keep costs down, spent a couple of nights with my wife's Aunt Mary and Uncle Roger, who lived in Anaheim Hills, maybe thirty minutes from the Magic Kingdom. Before embarking on the trip, I had spoken with one of my old fraternity brothers, Rick, who lived down in Southern Cal, and had reluctantly agreed to pay him a visit during the trip.

Compared to me, Rick had been through some tough times since graduating from college. A divorce from his college sweetheart, after not more than a year of marriage, had left him in somewhat of a fragile state. Of course, it didn't help that Rick almost single-handedly supported the Coors family with his penchant for beer. After the divorce and some alcohol-related trouble, Rick "saw the light," so to speak, and started attending church. He admitted to me that his original motivation was to meet women. But I don't think God cared what got Rick there, as long as he kept coming back. And boy, did he ever!

Not long after Rick was "born again," I started receiving phone calls from him. And while I enjoyed reconnecting with my Sigma Chi "big brother," his zeal for evangelism put a bit of a damper on the calls. I would listen for thirty to forty minutes, inserting the occasional "uh huh" to signal that I had not hung up the phone yet. Then I would politely draw the conversation to a close with a halfhearted explanation of why I was comfortable in my relationship with God. Honestly, I wasn't close to God anymore, but implying that I was, allowed me to end each phone call with him politely.

The plan was that after our first day at Disneyland, I would drive out to Rick's home in Corona and have dinner with him. The drive down Interstate 91 from Anaheim Hills to Corona was not a long one, and the traffic was not bad on a Saturday evening either. I arrived at Rick's house to a big bear hug and a cold can of Coors, which surprised me just a tad. *Christians drink beer?* I thought. Rick threw some steaks on the grill, and over a few beers we caught up on each other's lives in the years since college. Of course, Rick shifted into his evangelistic mode as the evening progressed, but sitting with him there face-to-face, his message didn't seem quite as intimidating as it did on the phone. (It was either that or the cumulative effects of the beer.)

Aware of the late hour, and the reality of a drive back on a route I wasn't entirely familiar with, I told Rick that I needed to get going. I thanked him for dinner, gave him a big hug, and let him know how great it was to see him. Rick and I had always shared a special bond, and seeing him again reminded me of that. I was still not quite comfortable with Rick's gentle but persistent pushing, but the awkwardness that I had felt in our phone calls over the years had subsided somewhat. I drove away, vowing to keep in touch and to think about what he had shared with me.

Heading down the freeway, my head and heart were a bit unsettled as I considered the message that Rick had delivered. It seemed like finding God had made a world of difference for him after all the struggles that he had been through in his life. But that was what Rick needed, not me; I was in control of my life. My life was going along just perfectly: good career, a beautiful wife, two healthy children, a house in the suburbs, etc., etc. Yet something was stirring inside of me. After all, much of what Rick was selling I had already bought many years before. I just didn't agree with everything that he had proposed. I knew God was in my heart, but I just hadn't felt the need to pay Him much attention in the years since high school.

What happened next is still as clear in my head as my retreat experience with God. I had decided that the only way to settle the answers that were swirling in my head was to put the question up to the big man Himself. And so, as I cruised along the highway, I said a quick and simple prayer that went something like this: "God, I want to believe in you, but I'm just not sure. Sometimes in my life I have placed my faith in you, but I don't know for sure. So, if you could just give me a sign ... " At that exact moment, I reached the top of a winding uphill stretch of Interstate 91. There, I saw a brightly lit cross perched atop a lone hill. It was almost as if someone had dropped the cross from above and hit the ground just as I finished my plea to God!

Many people, maybe most, would look at something like this and say that it was just a "coincidence." It was a coincidence that I just passed by a particular spot, at a certain time, while focusing on that specific thought and looking up just at the right moment, etc. But that is not how coincidences really work.

A coincidence is when you exit the freeway into a town that you have never been in before, while saying to yourself, "Boy a cheeseburger sounds excellent right now!" Then, just as you turn the corner at the bottom of the ramp, you suddenly spot the familiar red and yellow marquee for In-N-Out Burger. That is a coincidence. Or maybe you order a Double-Double with fries and a shake, which comes to $9.79, and you dump the contents of your pocket on the counter to reveal two shiny quarters, two dimes, one nickel and four pennies: exactly seventy-nine cents! Or maybe the cashier gives you your receipt and says, "Your number is eleven," and you muse how that was your jersey number in Little League and high school soccer! Those are coincidences.

If we are looking for coincidences, we can find them everywhere. Merriam-Webster's defines coincidence as "the occurrence of events that happen at the same time by accident but seem to have some connection." And the entry on Wikipedia for coincidence starts out like this: "Coincidence is the noteworthy alignment of two or more events or circumstances without obvious causal connection." Seen in that light, the fact that my receipt number at a fast-food restaurant matches my high school jersey number amounts to one thing and one thing only: a coincidence. There is no connection between the receipt and my jersey, and my having worn number eleven did not cause my receipt to come out of the register right after ten and just before twelve.

By contrast, what happened on Interstate 91 was not a coincidence. When I prayed earnestly to God to "give me a sign," He did just that, with a visual that I would understand and at a time where my heart was open to hearing His voice. A car accident could have gotten my attention just as easily, but I would not have attributed it to the prayer I just made.

As I stated previously, I believe in my heart that God is always communicating with us on some level. He speaks to us through the beauty of His creation, through His words in the Scriptures, through dreams, through people that we meet, and yes, even with a lighted cross by the side of the freeway.

And so, the question that I continue to ask is, how often are we listening? How often do we allow our hearts to be open to what He has to say to us? Sadly, even with the experiences I have had, the answer for myself has been—not often enough. Fortunately, sometimes God opens our hearts while we are not awake.

CHAPTER 8

CALIFORNIA DREAMIN'

"I will listen to what God the Lord says; he promises peace to his people, his faithful servants—but let them not turn to folly." (PSALM 85: 89 NIV)

arlier, I talked about the dream that had led me to begin writing this book. Unlike some, I have been a dreamer all my life. By dreamer, I don't mean someone who sits around imagining what the world might be like if only this or that would happen. Rather, I mean that I have always had a very active and vivid dream life at night while I sleep. Many people say that they don't dream or can't remember their dreams. This always strikes me as very odd, because I have no trouble recounting my dreams and I still have a vivid picture of them in my head for hours after I have woken.

When I was younger, I used to have a recurring dream that I was being left behind by my family. I am not just talking about a recurring theme in my dreams that my family was going somewhere without me. That was true, too, but here I mean that I had the same exact dream time after time.

In the dream, my family and I are at my grandparents' house, and we are all out on the sidewalk saying goodbye after the visit. We are all dressed in our "Sunday best" with costumes suggesting a time in the early 1900s (and no, I'm not that old!). The women and girls wear ankle-length dresses, and the men look like they could be in a barbershop quartet. As my father pulls up to the curb in our convertible sedan with a jump seat in the back, I see a dirty stream of water running down the gutter between the rest of us and the car. As my brothers and sisters get into the car, my grandmother, who is afraid that I will get my clothes dirty if I step over the curb, is quietly restraining me. And as I stand there straining against my grandmother's clutch, my family drives off down the street with smiles plastered on their faces and hands raised, waving goodbye. I begin to cry, convinced that I am seeing the last glimpse of my family. Fortunately, as is the case with dreams, I wake up.

In fact, I used to have several different recurring dreams besides this one. They always had to do with being separated from my mother and father and being able to see but not reach them. My dad left us when I was about six years old, and no doubt this had something to do with my dreams of abandonment in later years.

I still remember vividly the day my father told me he was leaving. I was rolling around the house on one of those little riding toys that kids have. It was a purple Dino, from the Flintstones cartoon, and belonged to my younger brother David. My mom and dad were talking in the kitchen of our row house in the officers' quarters at St. Albans, Naval Hospital in New York where my dad was doing his residency. As I rolled by, my dad called me in and explained that he was leaving. He said that he was going to a place called Vietnam, where there was a war going on, and that he would work on a hospital ship. He assured me he wouldn't be leaving for a month, but said that Vietnam was far away, and I wouldn't see him for a long time. To the best of my ability as a six-year-old, I quietly listened to my mom and dad, rolling back and forth on Dino as they spoke.

Without a word, I then maneuvered backward and out into the hall-way, the plastic wheels of my dinosaur friend clicking in unison on the hardwood floor. I parked at the screen door where I stared out into the yard … and cried. I remember my dad coming up behind me and holding on to me tight and telling me that everything would be alright. After all, he was just leaving for a little while, and he would be back. Yet something inside my tiny heart told me there was more to it than that.

During the following month, we packed our belongings and headed to Maryland, where both sets of grandparents lived, as did cous-ins, aunts, and uncles. My dad was with us as we moved in and got settled into our new home, but left soon after to report for duty. I think I adapted to the new environment quickly, and I have many significant memories of the years we lived in Maryland. Our cous-ins lived just a few streets away, and the grandparents on my mom's side were only ten minutes away. I was at an age when I took a keen interest in sports, both as a fan and as an athlete, and was lucky to have two great professional teams in nearby Baltimore, the Colts and my beloved Orioles, a team I follow to this day. I can remem-ber practicing ground balls with my best friend Mike Athey in his backyard, pretending to be our favorite Oriole. And yet, despite all these delightful distractions, there was not a single day that I didn't yearn to be with my father.

I remember waking up on New Year's Day a year and a half later—I believe it was 1969—with the sense that something special would happen that day. As I shuffled through the cold house in my pajamas, I went down to the basement bedroom expecting to see Joe, who was an old college friend of my parents. Joe was my dad's best friend growing up and was something of an uncle to my siblings and me.

There had been a party at the house the night before, and I remember hearing the loud and celebratory voices that accompanied the New Year and the alcohol that came with it. Peeking tentatively into the still dark room, I saw the hulking shape of a man curled up in the bottom bunk bed. It wasn't Joe. It was my beloved father! As the tears flowed freely down my cheek, my dad picked me up and held me in his arms, much like the day he told me he was leaving. But these were tears of joy. My father, whom I had longed to be with for so long, was home now. Even as I write this today, there are tears streaming down my face as I remember this joyful reunion.

My joy would be short-lived, however, as we learned over the next couple of days that dad would not be staying long. He was moving to California, and while he would still be my father, he and mom would not be married anymore. Maybe that is when the dreams started. I honestly don't know, but my guess is that dreams of abandonment have been the norm for the millions of young boys whose fathers or mothers have left them. In my studies and reading over the years, I have come to understand the toll that fatherlessness has on families, cultures, societies, and the world. I have gained an intellectual understanding of the pain and dysfunction created by absentee fathers that I personally experienced as a young boy and well into my adult years.

Dreams say something about us. They say something about our fears, about our pain, about our longings. They say things about our regrets for the past, but they also say things about our hopes for the future. I believe God uses dreams to speak to our hearts and to share with us His plan for us, His vision of the men and women that we can become.

Thankfully, I rarely have those abandonment dreams anymore. Gone also are the melancholy dreams about the "good old days"—those times in my life that I look back on with fond memories and yearn for. I used to wake from that kind of dream with such a sense of longing that the tears that started while I was in my dream state and was preparing to leave some person or place would continue flowing after I was awake. I do still wake up sometimes with tears in my eyes, but now those tears come with a sense that God has some message for me.

A couple of years back, I awoke from a dream in just that state of awareness that God was speaking. The dream came two weeks before the annual men's retreat at the church I attend. I had been very active in the leadership of our men's ministry, and the retreat had become the pinnacle of the year for me. I had attended my first retreat four or five years earlier, at one of the darkest times in my life. At the time, I knew hardly anyone from the church but had this powerful sense that I needed to go, that I needed to connect with some other men— men who might help me in a time where I thought everything was slipping away from me. To this day, I look back at that first men's retreat as one of the catalysts that saved my marriage. It revived my spiritual life and set me on a new course.

In the dream, I am at a business conference in some city in some nondescript foreign country. Walking out of the convention center to head back to my hotel, I strike up a conversation with a young Asian woman who had attended the same conference. As we crossed the street, the young woman suddenly morphs into my youngest daughter, Erin.

As we continue our walk, the surrounding environment looks more and more run-down, in a way that is typical of many large cities, where shiny glass buildings are a short walk from concentrations of poverty and homelessness. Suddenly, a man who is standing in front of a small newsstand steps out in front of me and starts to rant loudly about the world ending or some other apocalyptical message. Fearing for the safety of Erin, I immediately go on the offensive and with both hands grab the man by the collar of his jacket and shout into his face that if he does not back off, I will hurt him badly. Almost immediately, the man shrinks back down within himself, giving off an air of fear and terror that quickly brings a feeling of regret to my heart—regret that I could treat another human being, even in defense of myself and daughter, in such an outwardly aggressive way.

As I apologize to the man for my behavior, I notice out of the corner of my eye that my young daughter has wandered into an empty lot that is strewn with broken bottles, disabled shopping carts, and homeless men huddled under newspapers and boxes. As I move quickly to cut her off, she kneels and strokes the head of an African man whose appearance reminds me of the pictures we see in the media of hunger-stricken areas of that continent. Seeing the tenderness in her touch but gripped by a sense of danger, I kneel next to her and tell her we need to be going. "But Daddy, he needs help!" she says to me, and I begin to weep.

When I woke up from that dream with tears streaming down my face, I was confused. God has spoken to me through this dream, I thought, but was not sure just exactly what He was trying to tell me. I know that there are tremendous needs in third-world countries. We see and hear of them every day. People suffer from poverty and malnutrition in 95 percent of the world. Here, we live in two-story homes, drive nice cars, and have no clue what hunger is. I often stop myself when I utter the phrase "I'm starving!" and think how asinine it sounds. But I know also that there are needs here as well.

There are thousands, if not millions, of men in this country who will go to bed at night experiencing a different poverty. It might not be as visible as the worn face or distended stomach of someone who is dying of starvation, but it is a poverty of the soul. The poverty that comes from a father's abandonment, harsh words, or beatings, the poverty that says to a child, "You are not worth it. I do not love you." It is a poverty that creates alcoholism and drug addictions and other attempts to self-medicate our wounds and our pain. It is a kind of soul poverty that replicates itself in one generation after another.

That night, I began a dialogue with God.

"God, I am confused right now. What do you want me to do?"

He replied, "Take care of my men."

"But I know that there are men all around me who need help just as much as those in poorer countries need help. Which ones do you want me to help?"

God replied, "It doesn't matter."

At that point, a floodgate of tears opened.

I knew what God wanted me to do, but I wasn't sure where He wanted me to do it. Was God telling me I needed to sell all my earthly possessions and move my family to an impoverished part of the world to take care of the downtrodden? This is a question I kept asking myself. Pictures and stories about the work of our church's missionaries often evoked this feeling in me. Wanting to see if God's plan for me was to be a missionary, I took part in a mission trip to Laos that someone in my men's group organized. To be sure, it was a great experience, but it also left me with a simple message that God was not calling me into the foreign mission field. Once again, God had given me a very specific answer to my prayer!

How do I know it was God speaking to me? How do I know I was not just hearing my own pent-up emotions and feelings of guilt? I knew it was God, because if I had answered my questions with pre-programmed thoughts, the response would have been: "Help the poor in Africa. They need it more." Of course, my human thinking was subject to the half-truths and biases that come with growing up in America, where everything is in abundance and the perception is that money and material things are enough to care for anyone's needs. God bases His answers on the truth that we are all needy and that He doesn't play favorites.

I have learned firsthand through my work in men's ministry that there are plenty of hurting and needy men in our country, cities, neighborhoods, and even our churches!

MY "FORTY YEARS IN THE DESERT"

¹⁴"For all who are led by the Spirit of God are sons of God."
(ROMANS 8:14 NIV)

Sometimes the experiences that God uses to communicate with us don't fully unfold in a three-hour visit with a friend or in the instant that we take to turn a corner and see a lighted cross. Sometimes we take weeks, months, or even years to fully comprehend that He has been speaking to us through an experience or chain of events. We get so wrapped up in our day-to-day lives and the rhythms of the world that we don't stop to consider that what we are going through, whether it is sensational or mundane, might be our Father trying to get our attention. In our churches, we come to believe that God only gets involved with us when something large needs to happen. We only sit up and take notice when something spectacular happens to us or someone we know, or when we see some big happening in the media. We wait for the stories or vignettes that make us stand up and say, "Praise the Lord!"

The God I know is a God of the common man. We tend to focus on Moses, Abraham, Joshua, Job, and other giants of the faith. In fact, most of the heroes of the Bible—including some of the above men—led a good portion of their lives as extremely average persons. What set them apart was that when they were called by God, they swallowed their pride (or squelched their fears) and answered the call. A phrase that I have heard in many sermons and read in many Christian inspirational books over the years goes something like this: "God uses ordinary people to accomplish extraordinary things." While somewhat trite, this is the truth. But before He can use us ordinary folk to accomplish extraordinary things, He needs to get our attention, and then He needs to give us some orientation for our journey.

The bursting of the dotcom bubble certainly got my attention, but even then, it took me a while to hear God's voice and reorient my life. In mid-2001, I thought I was firmly ensconced in the high-tech world. I had been at the same company for seven and a half years, which in that industry is like a lifetime. My time there spanned the early years of the Internet and the beginnings of what would come to be known as the dotcom industry. These were years when loyalty to a company usually was cast aside as people hopped around from start-up to start-up, lured by lucrative stock options that promised overnight riches. But I was happy where I was. The company had an excellent culture and seemed to be doing well. I thoroughly enjoyed my work and loved the people I worked with. As I came to understand a few years later, however, I had become too comfortable in my life. God's goal is to push us out of our comfort zone, and out of my comfort zone is precisely where I spent the better part of the next decade. When we believe we are fully self-sufficient and everything is going well, we have no need for God—or at least He allows us to believe that for a time!

I had never intended to get into the world of high technology, at least not in a technical capacity. After flailing around in college for seven years, sampling three schools and three different majors, I finally graduated with a bachelor's degree in, of all things, advertising. It would be easy to say that I had studied advertising out of a desire to exercise my creative side. But for most of my life, I had tried to convince myself that I didn't have a creative bone in my body. It took me until I was well into my thirties to understand that creativity comes in all different forms and that you are not devoid of creativity just because you can't do a charcoal sketch or play flamenco guitar.

The truth of the matter is that the girl I was smitten with, a sorority girl in the Delta Gamma house, was an advertising major. And I figured that changing my degree would mean more time with her. What the heck? I had transferred to San Jose to follow my girlfriend a few years earlier, so changing my major didn't seem nearly as crazy as that. Besides, I figured I was going to marry this girl anyway, and maybe we could start an advertising agency together!

Moving to a new city or changing college majors just to be close to a love interest is probably not the smartest thing in the world. I did it twice and lost the girl both times! Maybe the fact that I repeated my folly was a sign of my neediness. I was kind of like the lost puppy dog that will follow you home if you are friendly enough to bend down and scratch his ears. However, no matter how cute the puppy dog is and how pitiful he looks standing there at your doorstep, you eventually realize you probably shouldn't keep him. Besides, most girls don't want a long-term thing with a man who is overly needy! They want a white knight in shining armor—either that, or the quarterback of the football team.

But this part of the story isn't about girls, knights, or quarterbacks. This part is about a decision I made that signaled the beginning of what I would come to think of as my "forty years of wandering in the desert" (a Biblical reference to the extra time God made His people take to enter the Promised Land). While that period of my life has long since ended, I have become more and more convinced that my lot in life will include a lot more wandering. It is another way that God speaks to and through us.

At work, my company was embarking on a new focus on quality known as "Six Sigma," and they had chosen me to go through the training and certification process for it. This was based on my involvement in many business-process improvement projects around the company. Six Sigma is a philosophy that seeks to transform the decision-making process in business into one that is based heavily on data and statistics. I had never seen myself as a statistics type of guy, but once I got into the training, I enjoyed it. I had been in the corporate world long enough to understand the unhealthy roles politics, personalities, and ambition play in making business decisions, and I was ready for a much more scientific approach. The training consisted of a series of five-day intensive off-site meetings every five to six weeks, culminating in a certification test that would give me the right to call myself a "Six Sigma Black Belt."

On the Friday afternoon before the last week of training, the director of our group called my boss and me into his office for an unscheduled meeting. In somewhat conciliatory tones, he informed me that the "Process Excellence" team, which sponsored the company's Six Sigma efforts, was being put on hold because of some changes in senior management. Then came the zinger. My project was being canceled and my position was being eliminated. He was quick to assure me it had nothing to do with my performance or value to the group; it was just the result of an organizational decision. He was also quick to assure me that they would help me find another position in the department or somewhere else in the company if I wanted to continue in a different capacity.

God was moving in my life, but I had no clue that He was. He certainly didn't send me an email memo revealing His intentions. I remember hearing a sermon a while back where the pastor gave his explanation for why God did not provide us with the ability to see into the future. He said that if we had a picture of what God's plan for us was, we would run as fast and as far as we could in the opposite direction, because the plan would scare the hell out of us! Now, that's not to say that God's plans for us truly are things we should run from—quite the opposite! What I'm saying is that if we had a crystal ball with which we could investigate and watch our lives unfold over one, two, five, or ten years, then our human nature would focus on the hard things. We would skim right past all the good times and the blessings, zero in on the times of pain and suffering, and say, "I'm not signing up for that!" In doing so, we would never get to the place that God wants us to be, and we would miss a lot of cool things along the way.

Consider this scenario: You are planning to go to a reunion in Rhode Island one summer, and you live in San Francisco. Airfare for a whole family being what it is, you figure that driving is the way to go. You take out a map to plot out the drive from California to the East Coast. Looking at the map of the United States, you see that you would have to travel across hundreds of miles of desert to reach your destination. You also notice that a fair amount of the journey would take you through some winding roads and high mountain passes. And you conclude that there would also be a whole lot of nothing between the cities and towns along the way. Then you figure out the costs involved in driving cross-country: gas, motels, food and drink, maybe tolls. And after reviewing the route and calculating the actual cost, you might think to yourself that driving is not worth the headaches, even though flying is still out of the question. So, you stay home. Sadly, what you did not factor in are the great times you might have with your family in Rhode Island, never mind some of the great experiences you might have getting there by car. All that you focus on is the burden of travel!

Pain, as I understand it, is a gift that God has given to us. Pain is a gift that we can certainly try to decline, and I stress the word *try*. But ultimately it is a gift that allows us to become who we are. It builds our character, it gives us confidence, and in the end, it protects us. We've all heard the maxim, phrased in one form or another, "What doesn't kill you can only make you stronger." Most anyone can look back on some painful experience or hard time and admit that they came out better because of it.

But aren't there some obvious exceptions to this rule? How about the person who, because of a horrific accident, spends the rest of their life tied to a wheelchair? Or how about the person who is born or stricken with an incurable disease? How are they stronger? These examples merit serious consideration, and we must be sure never to downplay someone else's suffering.

The thing to understand about the maxim "What doesn't kill you can only make you stronger" is that it hinges on a small three-letter word: can, c-a-n. Adversity can make us stronger, if we choose to allow it. We always have a choice in life. We can decide to let pain debilitate us, or we can work to use it positively.

Let's face it: pain is a part of life. It comes with being human and living on this earth. We cannot avoid pain any more than we can avoid laughter. Both happen because we are alive. Many first-time parents go into parenthood with the misguided idea that they can somehow set things up just right—take just the right precautions or buy just the right products—to "guarantee" that their child will never experience pain. But as they come to find out, usually within days or weeks of the baby's arrival, there is no accident-free world, and there is no escaping pain. What they also learn is that with each accident, each broken bone, and each skinned knee comes learning and growth. The burned and blistering hand, painful as it is, teaches the child that putting their hand in the fire is something to be avoided!

And so, I faced my pain at work. I faced the pain attached to "Your position is being eliminated." The pain that came with the thought that, despite being told that it had nothing to do with my performance, I couldn't help but feel like they were just saying that to be nice. It must have something to do with my performance; maybe I wasn't as smart, creative, or as valuable to the company as I thought I was. Maybe it was being called a "business decision" to let me down gently. Looking back on it now, I believe that it truly was just a business decision, one that would signal the start of my wandering in the desert.

After I had gotten over the initial shock of losing my job, I looked at the turn of events as an opportunity to do something else. As much as I liked the company that I worked for, loved the people, and was proud of my contributions, I was ready for a change in my life. I was correct about the need for change, but my idea of change and God's idea of change turned out to be two radically different things. I told my boss that I would look at a couple of positions in the group that seemed like they might be good fits, but in my mind, I had already accepted the severance package. It was time for me to leave.

We had booked a big family vacation to Hawaii with three other families. The fact that I would be unemployed after we returned did not remotely make me think of canceling the trip. To the contrary, one of the first things I did after resigning was to call the travel agent and extend the trip by an additional three days. Why not! I had an extremely generous severance package, which amounted to almost six months of income. I also had already planned a ten-day trip to Chile to attend my twenty-five-year high school reunion in November of that year. Thus, my "plan" was to take six months off, travel, and then go find a new job.

What I didn't plan for was the rest of 2001. The high-tech industry, which had been so good to me over the years, was already showing signs of a meltdown. The events of September 11, 2001, came just weeks after my job ended. These things coming together created a "perfect storm" that sunk my near-term employment prospects.

What I also did not know was that God had finally grown weary of trying to get my attention. He'd tried the gentle whispers and the little nudge, and even the proverbial two-by-four upside the head. Heck, He'd put up a lighted cross right before my eyes in answer to a direct challenge. But I just wasn't listening. I had walked away from the God of my youth, and He had been trying to reach me for twenty-five-plus years.

We all have this vision of how life is supposed to unfold, don't we? We get so busy with our dreams, goals, and plans, that we put blinders on and keep charging in the same direction, no matter what is going on around us and inside of us. We think of failure and unhappiness as gauges that tell us we need to become more disciplined, try a different approach, or work harder on our plan. Rarely do we see them as signs that maybe our plan is the problem.

Remember the man on the roof, pleading with God while the flood waters rise? The man had a definition of how things were supposed to go. He had a picture in his mind of how God was going to save him from drowning. Anything that didn't match his view of God—even a rescue helicopter—was just a distraction.

I titled this chapter "My 'Forty Years in the Desert'" in somewhat of a tongue-in-cheek manner. I've never actually been in a desert for more than a few hours, and my journey, at least until now, has been far less than forty years. I just thought it was a suitable metaphor to help me understand and explain to others the orientation that God has taken me through over these last few years. There have been plenty of moments of inspiration surrounded by long periods of aimless wandering. Through it all, God has been speaking, even if I wasn't always listening.

CHAPTER 10

WE'LL TRY IT
YOUR WAY

¹²"For the word of God is living and active, sharper than any two-edged sword, piercing to the division of soul and of spirit, of joints and of marrow, and discerning the thoughts and intentions of the heart." (HEBREWS 4:12)

As my extended vacation wound down and the "go back to work" portion of my plan was quickly approaching, I was very much wandering in the desert. Even if I had wanted to go back to work in a high-tech position, the jobs were not there. Besides, I had left my last job with a romantic notion that when it was time to go back to work, I would do something that I wanted to do, as opposed to just getting a job. The problem was that I had no clue of what I was going to do.

For years, I had struggled with where my career had taken me. Anger, frustration, and a feeling of being confined to a career path that I had never intended to go down ate at me on almost a daily basis. It wasn't the work per se; it was more of a question of personal fulfillment. "Is this really my calling?" I asked myself. One of my constant refrains whenever my wife and I would get into a heated argument, usually about money or the children, was, "When do I get to do what I want to do with my life?!" My wife Lori is one of those rare and blessed people who figured out what they wanted to do with their lives at a relatively early age. She discovered in high school that early childhood development was her passion, and she never looked back. All her schooling and most of her part-time jobs were done to support her vision of owning and operating a Montessori school with her older sister Debbie. It is a vision that has served Lori and our family well for over thirty-five years.

By contrast, I am one of those tortured souls who will probably go to their graves still trying to figure out what they want to do when they "grow up." I am grateful for the opportunities that a high-tech career has afforded me; it's just that I have never experienced in my work the joy and the passion that my wife has known over the years. Designing a better way to track defects in a piece of software or making sure that the software will ship on time just doesn't compare to helping a child learn to read or seeing that child years later as they graduate from college, knowing that you had some part in their success.

Sure, my career has been much more lucrative than my wife's, but not nearly as fulfilling. And for a long time, that bugged the hell out of me. So, "When do I get to do what I want to do with my life?!" became a refrain that gnawed at me like a Top 40 hit you can't get out of your head. Every time you turn on the radio or change station, there it is. The song might have a catchy tune or maybe some lyrics that grab your attention, but it becomes an instant irritation as soon as you hear the first few notes.

As a father of three, I can relate to the picture of God as a parent and a loving father. The joys and frustrations that I have felt with my kids. All the dilemmas that I have faced in trying to raise them. This is what God deals with as well. All the tears and smiles that I have experienced trying to be a loving father are like the ones that He experiences each day with you and me.

As parents, we try our best to prepare our kids for the world, knowing that at some point they will be on their own. They will make their own choices, and choices always have consequences. Eventually, our children will be on their own to fail and succeed, and to experience the joys and pain that come with those victories and defeats. We teach them, talk to them, lecture them, scold them, discipline them, and try to ground them in our values, all in the hope of equipping them to lead happy and well-adjusted lives. We don't give them everything they ask for, because we know some things are not safe, or are even dangerous for them. Shiny objects are intriguing to young children, but we don't hand them the butcher knife just because they asked for it.

Sometimes, though, we give in, knowing that they are probably going to get their fingers burned, so to speak. Unless we handcuff them to their bedposts, we understand, we can't stop them, anyway. And so, we take a deep breath and pray like mad we won't have to utter the age-old line, "I told you so!" We just bite our tongues and deliver the message, "Okay, if you feel so strongly that you need to do this, then go ahead, but please be careful." From my perspective as a father, I can appreciate that God repeats those very words daily—and, truthfully, that is what He uttered to me the day I walked away from my job to strike out on my own.

In roughly four years, God not only said, "Okay," but He opened the doors to five different career opportunities, each of which I just knew would bring me the fulfillment I had been searching for over so many years. In somewhat rapid fashion, I tried my hand at: owning a small business … teaching in the public schools … working construction … working in a recruiting agency … and finally, being an independent computer consultant. Ultimately, all these career exercises were relatively brief, but God spoke to me through them in distinct ways and taught me things about myself that I would never have learned had I not gone down those paths.

Mostly, what I learned is that our motivation for why we do things is important. My motivation to start a business was because I thought it would bring financial independence and plenty of free time. Some of my closest friends had been running successful businesses for years and seemed to be reaping the benefits of their hard work. I saw their country club memberships, nice cars, extravagant vacations, and beautiful homes, and I wanted the same. What I didn't see—or, more accurately, what I ignored—were the years of hard work they had put in, the stress this had caused on their marriages and relationships with their children, and the things they had sacrificed to get where they were. I only saw what I wanted to see. But as the loving parent He is, God allowed me to go down this path of small business ownership, not to let me gain riches, but to teach me some things that until then I had been too hardheaded to understand.

I had developed this weird belief that if I just duplicated what my friends were doing, then I would get everything that they had. And once that happened, my life would be fulfilled: my wife would love and adore me, my kids would turn out wonderfully, and I finally would be in control of my life. So, God said to me, "Okay, let's try it your way for a while." And I was off to the races!

CHAPTER 11

MAUI *WHAT?*

³"The voice of the Lord is over the waters; the God of glory thunders, the Lord thunders over the mighty waters. ⁴The voice of the Lord is powerful; the voice of the Lord is majestic. ⁵The voice of the Lord breaks the cedars; the Lord breaks in pieces the cedars of Lebanon.

⁷The voice of the Lord strikes with flashes of lightning.
⁸The voice of the Lord shakes the desert;
    the Lord shakes the Desert of Kadesh.
⁹The voice of the Lord twists the oaks and strips
    the forests bare.
And in his temple all cry, "Glory!" (PSALM 29:3-5, 7-9 NIV)

was convinced that owning a business would start me down the path of fulfillment and enlightenment. The question then became, what kind of business? So, I retreated into my cave and began my search for the perfect business. I didn't have any notion of what kind of business I wanted to be in, no burning passions that screamed out to me. But I was realistic. I knew I didn't have the time or resources to build a business from scratch, and I didn't have the money to buy an existing one. The thought of a franchise business thus invaded my mind; it required less time and capital than those alternatives.

Before I knew it, I was the proud owner of a Maui Wowi franchise. Despite what the name might make you think of, I was *not* selling marijuana. Maui Wowi is a smoothie company. Its model at the time was centered on a mobile tiki hut that was to be dragged around to events like arts and wine festivals, dog shows, or NASCAR races, so that the throngs of attendees could buy tropical-blend smoothies. Maui Wowi also was venturing into shopping malls and small store-fronts, which is where I wanted to set up shop.

To finance the business, I had to cash out what little money remained in our stock portfolio after the dotcom bust and the shock of 9/11 and also take out a small home equity loan. Borrowing money to start a business was a move my wife Lori was very much against, but I somehow got her to come around. In retrospect, I don't think she agreed with it so much as she grew tired of the constant badgering and assurances that I would offer about how I would never put the family in jeopardy. I remember one conversation in which she questioned the wisdom of betting our entire savings on a small business venture. "It's not like we would ever lose our house or anything like that!" I boldly (and arrogantly), replied, words I would soon come to regret.

The next few months brought with them a sense of both excitement and fear, which I think is natural during most significant life changes. The excitement of receiving the call confirming the acceptance of my application quickly turned to fear as I dropped a check for $25,000 into the mail. I then experienced the excitement of heading off to training at the corporate offices in Colorado, followed by the fear that maybe I had made a mistake after all. And there was the excitement of booking my first event, a large four-day NASCAR race in Sonoma, California, which promised crowds of over 100,000 over a three-day period. And with that came the fear that my equipment, which was fully paid for but almost two weeks late, might not arrive in time to do the event. I experienced the joy of seeing my equipment being loaded onto a rented flatbed trailer just one day before the event and then experienced the terror of nearly dumping my new equipment into a ravine on the narrow delta roads leading to the raceway. Finally, I was thrilled to take in over $3,600 cash over a three-day period, but soon realized that my expenses for the weekend were $3,800!

Okay, I reasoned, I made a few mistakes with my first event. But, with the ability to bring in that kind of revenue in just three days, my prospects looked promising. What I conveniently ignored was the fact that, over the five days that surrounded the event, I had driven more than 800 miles and averaged four hours of sleep per night— just to lose those $200! I did not even know when my next money-making gig would arrive, since I had spent all my time and energy on that event and hadn't had the chance to secure another one. Half-way through the summer, I discovered, the high-volume events in my area had already come and gone. Not yet discouraged, I started on the next part of the plan: securing a permanent location. I hoped to find a spot in a high-traffic shopping mall where lots of people would pass by every day. The cycle of hope and disappointment con-tinued. It was mostly happening too quickly for my young business mind to process, but eventually some lessons were learned.

Sometimes the lessons were costly, and sometimes they were just les-sons. For instance, I learned that when you sign a lease in a mall, you agree to be open 100 percent of the time the mall itself is open. This might not seem like a big deal when you read the lease, but it is a big deal when you get a call at 10:30 in the morning from mall secu-rity on one of the very few days you had planned to take off. The call was a friendly warning that my location was sitting dark and unat-tended thirty minutes after the mall had opened. I also learned that this was the third such incident that month, and that I was in dan-ger of being fined by the mall the next time it happened! The third time? I just assumed that my seventeen-year-old employees always showed up for work on time … and always came dressed in a clean uniform … and always aspired to do their very best to bring in lots of money for the business. After all, hadn't I given them the speech about how this was their business, too, and how I would reward them as the revenues grew? What I learned is that the only part they heard was about it being their business. And naturally, as business owners, they were well within their rights to show up whenever they wanted, to give out free smoothies to friends, and when tips weren't so good, to make up the difference by reaching into the register. Yes, I learned lots of great lessons courtesy of Maui Wowi!

I'd like to say that, with all the learning, my business was growing, and profits were piling up within a matter of months. Money *was* rolling in, I was simply holding it for someone else who had a claim on my business. There was the mall landlord, the product suppliers, the utility companies, and my employees—all the people who had to get paid before I even opened the doors each day. At the end of the month, there just never seemed to be much left for me. And so, approximately five months after opening the franchise—the business that was going to put me on "easy street," the business that would not jeopardize my family's financial well-being, the business that was going to set me free—I closed the doors and retreated into my cave.

When I made the choice to go into business for myself, it was partially out of a sense of despair. Yes, there was this delusional voice in my head that said I was smart enough and talented enough, that all I had to do was pick a business, and things would just fall into place. And there was the misguided perception that money, and the things that money can buy, would give me the sense of peace that I had been (and have been) searching for all my life. Those things, and much more, contributed to my unwise decision to bet it all on a smoothie business called Maui Wowi. But ultimately, it was despair that drove me. Those words, "It was despair that drove me," usually precede " ... to drink," or " ... to have an affair," or maybe even " ... to rob a bank." In my case, my despair drove me to risk the financial well-being of my family and my relationship with my wife Lori on a feeling in my heart that told me I couldn't just go back to life as it had been before I lost my high-tech job.

Deep in my heart, I was longing for something different, and I thought that returning to the corporate world would kill me. I didn't think it would literally kill me, although people do die from stress-related heart attacks at work every day. But I did think that going back to what I had been doing for the previous fifteen years would be a signal of defeat. It would be a signal that I wasn't good enough or smart enough to make it on my own. Nobody ever actually said that I would be a failure if I surrendered and went back to work. In fact, most everyone encouraged it. But I have always been my toughest critic and could not stop the critic's accusations from ringing in my ears.

It never occurred to me that the cause of my despair had nothing to do with my line of work, what car I drove, or where I took my vacations. By the world's standards, I had been doing well in my high-tech job. I was living the American Dream, yet there was this increasing sense that something was missing in my life. No matter what I tried to fill that hole in my heart with, the feeling of despair just kept persisting; more than that, it kept intensifying. What God would ultimately teach me during my "forty years in the desert" was that the hole in my heart was God-shaped and only He could fill it. Until then, I kept wandering and searching, just as Moses had.

As I mentioned earlier, I've come to understand the hard times, the painful times, are what make us grow and define who we are. This sounds so trite, I realize, but it is a universal truth. When faced with pain and suffering, we have exactly two choices in life. We can bitch and moan about what a victim we are and how unfair life is, or we can just accept, as Forrest Gump did, that "shit happens" and keep on running.

When I closed the smoothie business down, the inconvenient reality facing me was that I had spent all our savings, still owed a bunch of people a bunch of money, had no income whatsoever, and was facing one of the bleakest jobs markets I had ever experienced. I was exhausted and honestly felt like I had come to the end of my rope. So, once again I retreated into my cave.

One day, while scrolling through another dead-end job search site, I came to a scary understanding. I could understand how a person, in the depths of despair, might consider suicide as an option. How when things got so bad and all seemed lost, one could believe that the best alternative was just to end their life. Truthfully, I never really contemplated suicide for myself, but the fact I could understand how others might choose that route acted as a wake-up call for me. It signaled to me that if I had not hit bottom already, I was very close to it. I think God put that shocking realization about suicide in my head to get my attention—and that He did. I was beginning to remember that I was not alone in the world, no matter how much it sometimes felt that way.

CHAPTER 12

GIVING UP ON THE DREAM

¹⁷"Consequently, faith comes from hearing the message, and the message is heard through the word about Christ." (ROMANS 10:17 NIV)

One thing that began stirring in my heart during my foray into the world of small business ownership was the desire to find a church where I felt comfortable. It had been five or six years since our family had been regular attendees at any church, although we had done some experimentation from time to time. With months, and sometimes years, between visits, we had tried out churches that friends, co-workers, and family members had urged us to visit. But the search was halfhearted, and we always seemed to find, even after just one visit, one or more reasons why a particular church did not work for us. And then some more time would pass, and the cycle would repeat itself.

My stirring was not so much about finding the perfect church and more about trying to recapture the sense that God was alive, real, and interested in what was going on in my life. God continued to whisper to me, to nudge me, but it was hard for me to hear or feel Him amid my despair. I didn't ignore the promptings as much as I squelched the voice and the messages that would enter my consciousness every so often. Somewhere along the line, I had come to the unstated conclusion that I was the master of my own destiny, even though I was quick to blame everyone but myself when things didn't work out.

When it came right down to it, I had let the busyness of my career and raising a family serve as excuses for not giving in to the promptings that I felt in my heart. My guiding force was not the creator of the universe; it was the pursuit of the American Dream. I now understand that this dream is a complete lie, which, if pursued long enough, will bring about the opposite of what it purportedly promises. It seems weird, or almost un-American, to say that the American Dream is a lie, doesn't it? Let me offer some more perspective.

I'm not saying that there is anything wrong with the values behind the American Dream, which, depending on where you get your definition, is the ideal that every U.S. citizen should have an equal opportunity to achieve success and prosperity through hard work, determination, and initiative. Unfortunately, what too many Americans believe is that success (usually defined financially) and prosperity (again, usually defined financially) always bring with them peace, joy, and a sense of fulfillment. My studies and my experience have shown, however, that the road to the American Dream is littered with prosperous people who are nothing short of miserable.

We had attended, from time to time, a nondenominational church in San Jose called WestGate Church. My sister-in-law Debbie and her husband Tim had been going there for a couple of years and spoke well of the church. My wife's grandmother had also attended there many years earlier, when it was called Saratoga Avenue Baptist. There was nothing special about the church, but because we had family ties there, it seemed a reasonable choice for our twice-a-year pilgrimages at Christmas and Easter.

I'll freely admit that the few times that I stepped into the church outside of the major holidays, I was not especially impressed—not by the pastor, the service, or even the music. Every time I attended a non-holiday service, I came away feeling like I had just fulfilled an obligation. I hadn't arrive thinking that I was merely checking off the "go to church on Sunday" box on my list of responsibilities, but that was exactly how I felt when I left. There was no inner stirring or joy, no "religious experience" to speak of.

What I left with on those rare Sundays was a judgmental spirit—*my* judgmental spirit. I knew I had a spiritual void that needed to be filled, but I would blame that fact on the pastor and his message, the worship team and their music, the building and the chairs—pretty much anything that drew the blame away from myself.

And yet something kept pulling me back. Something told my heart that it would be good for me to return to this place, this church called WestGate. And so I kept going back. It was there that God really got ahold of my heart and began to work in me in ways I never in my wildest dreams would have imagined.

"YOU BETTER SIT DOWN KIDS"

⁵"Every word of God is flawless; he is a shield to those who take refuge in him. ⁶Do not add to his words, or he will rebuke you and prove you a liar." (PROVERBS 30: 5-6 NIV)

E arly in my walk through the desert, I found myself gravitating more and more to Christian music. I noticed it had this uncanny ability to create a tightness in my chest, usually followed by a welling of tears in my eyes. While I don't play a musical instrument and am not a talented singer, my mom fostered in me a love of music from a relatively early age. I remember as a kid lying on the floor in the living room listening to the record player and belting out show tunes from my mom's favorite Broadway musicals.

During this early part of my wandering time, my sense of despair seemed to increase by the day. I was constantly looking for a cure. One day, while I sat at a stoplight, I noticed a bumper sticker on the car in front of me. The bumper sticker featured an image of a dove, big block letters spelling out "K-LOVE," and a radio station number. I changed the station to 91.9 and was quickly overwhelmed with emotions.

The song was called "Testify to Love," by a group called Avalon. They had popularized it on a show from the late 1990s called *Touched by an Angel*, which I had seen only once or twice. I don't know why, but the lyrics of that song cut straight into my heart. They penetrated me, and every time I heard the song, tears welled up in my eyes, reflecting the pain that I had buried for so long. What was it about this song, and some others I would encounter over the next few years, that had the power to bring me to tears?

Looking back over my younger years, I can only remember ever hearing two songs that brought me to tears. One of them, I am slightly embarrassed to admit, was a sappy song called "Mandy," by Barry Manilow, which was popular in my junior year of high school. My girlfriend Jennifer was a big Manilow fan and had the album playing the night I came over to say goodbye to her. She was going away with her family on an extended vacation of six-plus weeks, and this was the first time we would be apart since we had started dating.

Walking home that night, with the song ringing in my head, and with that touch of melancholy that usually comes when someone close to us leaves, I forced myself to cry! I think that in some ways I did so out of guilt, knowing that I *should* have been sad. In truth, I wasn't really feeling it. With my girlfriend out of the picture for the summer, I would be free to hang out with my buddies. Guilt is such a powerful motivator, and it can make us do some crazy things. For me that night, this meant singing "Mandy" repeatedly and forcing myself to cry. I know now, and I think I even knew then, that those tears were fake. I say this because I've heard the song dozens of times over the years since then and have not once come close to tears. Sometimes I will break out in a big grin as I think back and imagine what I must have looked like walking down that lonely street, my grief spilling out all over the place. The image brings to mind the phrase Charlie Brown made famous: "Good Grief!" Coincidentally, in my senior year I played the lead in the musical, *You're a Good Man Charlie Brown*, opposite none other than my girlfriend Jennifer, who played Lucy!

Back in the late sixties, there was a well-known radio hit called "You Better Sit Down Kids," which was a song that made me cry as a child. The singer was Cher, who later had a popular variety show on TV with her husband Sonny Bono. Interestingly, she sang the song from the perspective of a father who was sitting down with the children to tell them that mom and dad would not be married anymore and that, although he was leaving, he would still be their dad. It was an unusual song not just because Cher, a female singer, performed it, but also because divorce was a dirty little secret back then; it was not something that you talked about, let alone glorified in a song. I was maybe seven or eight years old when the song came out, and it jabbed a wound in me that was still open and fresh from when my mom and dad had sat me down a couple of years earlier for a very similar talk. Tears were the likely response for a child whose world had been torn apart by the subject matter of the song. I recently rediscovered the song on the online music service I subscribe to, and while it didn't reduce me to a puddle of tears, the lump in my throat instantly took me back to a time when I was a hurt and vulnerable boy. A sad boy crying by the speaker, hoping his daddy would come home. Music can do that for us.

And so, 91.9 FM became a permanent setting on my car radio dial. I honestly don't think I listened to any other station for six months to a year. God was now using music—or, more accurately, lyrics— to speak to me. And I was hearing Him loud and clear!

A song's message is so much more compelling when accompanied by splendid music. You are first drawn in by the music; maybe it's a catchy tune, an engaging melody, or a pleasant rhythm. Once it draws you in, you can't help but focus on the words that accompany it. Growing up, it was like a badge of honor to sing along, word for word, to a song that all your friends liked. And heaven forbid that you get some lyrics wrong, because your friends would ridicule you to no end! It wasn't enough to just listen to and enjoy the song; you had to know every word *and* be able to hit the cymbal on your "air drum" at just the right moment. The thing was, nobody was paying much attention to the totality of the words or what the artist might have been trying to say with them. It was just a bunch of words strung together and supported by guitars and drums.

Maybe it's simply a failing of the immature adolescent brain to stop and think that there might be a story or a message in the lyrics of a song. It's possible that teenagers are hesitant to take a break from music and reflect on the lyrics because doing so feels too much like a literature class in school where the teacher mandates that you analyze and comprehend the author's message rather than just appreciating it. This kind of exercise helps develop critical thinking and analytical skills, which are invariably important as kids step out into the world, but most kids in high school today want no part of that. Maybe schools would do their teens a favor if instead of William Shakespeare, they instead had them dissect the works of Snoop Dogg!

The thing I noticed as I listened to more and more Christian music was that besides the fact that the lyrics were speaking to my heart, the music was superb! The ever-growing stack of CDs in my car grew from the likes of Led Zeppelin, the Eagles, and Bob Dylan to groups like MercyMe, Casting Crowns, and the David Crowder Band. Don't get me wrong—I still love all that old "heathen" rock and roll music. While the irony is immediately apparent, I get a charge every time I hear "Highway to Hell" or "Hells Bells" from AC/DC. It's just darn good music!

What I found with Christian music, besides much cheerier topics than hell, was that the lyrics unleashed in me desires and feelings that I can only describe as life-giving and soul affirming. The lyrics for most songs always seemed to speak to me in a particular and profound way that considered what I was going through or struggling with at that moment. The lyrics gave me hope that there was an answer to the despair that I felt. It was as if someone knew precisely what I was going through and knew just the right words I needed to hear. And while I am not naïve enough to think that anyone wrote a song just for me, I cannot write off as "coincidence" the fact that a specific song played just when I needed to hear it. I believe God is a loving Father who senses when we are hurting and, in His wisdom, has just the right words to soothe our troubled hearts. I also believe that God can use absolutely anything to deliver those words to us when we need to hear them.

It's like God is a cosmic DJ with hundreds of millions of songs in His music library, and our hurts, fears, and the desires of our heart are transmitted across an intergalactic request line. God picks up the line, says, "I've got just the song for you!" and then spins the disc. I know all this because I have children of my own and I am continually thinking about how a particular song, book, sermon, news story or anecdote might speak to their hearts and, through its message, calm their fears or ease their pain.

In Matthew Chapter 7, Jesus talks about God as a generous parent: "Which of you, if his son asks for bread, will give him a stone? Or if he asks for a fish, will give him a snake? If you, then, though you are evil, know how to give good gifts to your children, how much more will your Father in heaven give good gifts to those who ask him!" (Matthew 7:9–11 NIV)

As a father of three adult children, I think of how much I desired to give them just what they needed, at just the right time. I think, too, of how many times I came up short in my attempts to give good gifts and instead left them with hurt or pain. In my heart, I wanted to deliver to them the right lyrics for the situation. I wanted them to hear the words and understand that their father, while speaking with a raised voice and sometimes even angrily, was attempting to display his love to them through those words. But as much as I try, my love for my children is imperfect. Though the desire is there, the execution often falls short. I know that my Father in heaven can deliver those words to His children with perfect timing, perfect delivery, and with the purest of intentions. I want to be that kind of father.

CHAPTER 14

DENIED
THREE TIMES

²⁶"In the same way, the Spirit helps us in our weakness. We do not know what we ought to pray for, but the Spirit himself intercedes for us through wordless groans. ²⁷ And he who searches our hearts knows the mind of the Spirit, because the Spirit intercedes for God's people in accordance with the will of God." (ROMANS 8:26-27 NIV)

Most of us go through life moving from one experience to the next without paying attention to what is going on inside and around us. In fact, most of us wouldn't even use the word "experiences" to describe the day-to-day routines of our lives. We get up in the morning and prepare for the day, just as we always do, and then head off to work, school, or play. It's true that most of the things we do during our days are not memorable, and many days we look back and can't remember anything at all. We use phrases like "It's all in a day's work" or "Another day, another dollar" and brush off questions like "How was your day?" with a halfhearted "Good. How was yours?" without giving it a moment of thought. Is life really that boring? Are most of our days such that we feel like there is nothing we want or need to share with anyone? Maybe a better question to ask is this: Were our lives meant to be so dull and nondescript?

This next story may appear trivial, but please stay with me. Some years back, I was going through a stretch of unemployment. At the time, jobs in my industry simply were not available. I live and work in the area of Northern California known as Silicon Valley, which was dealing with an economic slump brought on when the dotcom bubble burst. After many years of unprecedented growth in the high-technology sector, things had simply bottomed out. One of the biggest factors in this tech-specific downturn was that there had been so much investment money thrown at software companies that had nothing more than a creative idea. Such software came to be known as "vaporware"—the name says it all! Regardless of whether the business or product was actually viable, venture capital firms were throwing hundreds of millions of dollars at start-up companies that sometimes had little to show for themselves beyond a fancy website. It was like a feeding frenzy of sharks in a small tank, driven by the smell of blood. Recent college grads were receiving multiple six-figure offers simply because these start-ups, with millions to burn, needed to hire people. Job hopping from one start-up to another with the promises of sign-on bonuses and stock options became the norm for so many.

And then the bubble burst. Companies that were still in the concept stage shuttered as investors' patience and money ran dry. Even some companies that had brought worthwhile products to market and had generated some revenues were affected. To be sure, unlike the Great Recession of 2007–2009, the recession of the early 2000s was very contained. Stock brokerages and banks were not failing, countries were not defaulting, and major retailers were not vanishing. But this earlier recession hit high-tech industries especially hard. People in high-tech expected that the golden goose would be there forever, and when the goose died, it left many people out of work.

Given the prosperity that the high-tech world had created just a few years earlier, people in high-tech industries were sure that the world was ending! Gone were the days when hundreds of people, working for companies that produced nothing of substance, became instant millionaires when their companies went public. Gone were the days when someone could command obscene amounts of money and gobs and gobs of stock options just because they had a degree, a resume, and knew what a "browser" was. And gone were most of the jobs—at least the kinds of jobs that paid anywhere near what I had been earning.

While I was able to find some sort of employment during most of the three or four years that it took for the industry to rebound, there were periods of time when I spent most of my days surfing the internet in search of jobs that just weren't there. One morning, after yet another fruitless search, I decided the only way to keep from going stir-crazy was to go out into the warm spring air and get some exercise, which for me meant hitting the greens. Golfing then was a luxury, but one that I figured, through some twisted logic, that I deserved. And so, I set out for the local municipal golf course for a little exercise.

It was a beautiful spring day, and for whatever reason, I had this sense of peace about the day ahead of me. As I pulled into the parking lot of the golf course, one of my favorite contemporary Christian songs was playing on the radio. I cut the engine, and just listened. When the song ended, I turned off the radio and sat for another couple of minutes surveying the colors of spring that were splashed before my eyes. With the words of the song still ringing in my ears, I bowed my head and said a prayer, thanking God for the beautiful day and the opportunity to get out and do something that I enjoyed. And then I asked Him to join me! As I walked from my car towards the pro shop, my golf bag slung over my shoulder, I had this sense that today would be a special day. And boy was it!

When I play golf, it's usually a last-minute decision. I just show up, put my name on the standby list, and go hang out on the practice putting green, waiting to hear my name called. When someone who had a reservation doesn't show up, they call the next person on the list. The higher you are on the list, the less time hanging out on the putting green.

You don't get to choose your golfing partners this way, so you end up meeting lots of interesting folks. Once, my teenage son Thomas and I went out to the local municipal course and put our names on the list. A short wait later, we were called to the pro shop and informed we were to join the twosome already on the tee. It was a couple of old guys who, we learned, lived down the street from us. When we got home that afternoon, Thomas couldn't contain himself as we walked in the door, where his mom (my wife!) Lori greeted us.

"Hey boys, how was your golf game today?" she asked, giving Thomas a big hug.

Trying to suppress a grin that would soon turn to laughter, he said with a straight face and the polished timing and delivery of a stand-up comic, "Pretty good, but we played with a couple of real Dicks!"

"Thomas, that's not very nice!" Lori scolded him, stepping back with a look of shock on her face.

"But Mom," Thomas quickly replied, "they *were* both Dicks. Both of their names were Dick!" It turns out our golfing mates for the day were both blessed with the first name of Richard!

This day, however, I had arrived at the course with Jesus by my side. After all, I had asked Him to go golfing with me. The calm and serenity that had come over me earlier in the morning and the song ringing in my head put me in a rhythm that I've only experienced a handful of times in my life. Athletes refer to it as "being in the zone."

I hit a long and straight drive to start the day, but followed it up with a flubbed shot. Ordinarily, a string of four-letter words would have come next, but today seemed different. I recovered after the bad shot and vowed not to let any future bad shots get to me.

Without boring you with a shot-by-shot narrative of the rest of the day, I'll just say that I played out of my mind for the next thirteen and a half holes. Sure, I hit a bad shot now and then, but when I did, it was immediately followed by a miraculous recovery. Drive after drive found the middle of the fairway. I executed shots out of the sand traps with a mastery seen only on the PGA Tour. Putts were dropping into the cup from long distances with a frequency that defied statistical odds. It was almost embarrassing just how easy I was making it look—and in some ways, it *was* easy.

I hadn't asked Jesus to carry my bag, but I felt like He was carrying me! I just kept humming the tune from the radio in my head and thanking the Lord for every excellent shot that I made. Never had I played to the level I was at that day. Still, as the day wore on, I kept waiting for the bottom to drop out. I was waiting for something to go wrong, but nothing did.

Somewhere along the line, I thought to myself that absolutely nothing could ruin the magical day which I was experiencing. There was just this sense of calm in, and around, me that God had blessed me that day with the best golf game of my life. Of course, there was also the part of me that wanted to be in control of the outcome, and so I did mental math to assure me that, indeed, this would end up as my best score ever. Not merely content to just enjoy the gift that God had given me thus far, I set my sights on that target score, which surely would win me the esteem of pretty much everyone that I knew.

When, with just five holes to play, I hit an errant shot into some low-hanging trees, I figured my string of good holes was done. But again, a miraculous shot from under the trees kept the string alive.

My emotions were all over the place, and so were my conversations with God. As I glided to the next tee amidst a flurry of high fives, my prayers (and arrogance) continued to grow and I issued a serious (but foolish) challenge: "Lord, you could strike me with lightning right now, and it wouldn't ruin this day!" At the same time, I was also suffering from superstitious athlete syndrome, so I tried to hedge my bets in every kind of way. I said to myself, "Keep yourself humble ... Don't think too far ahead ... Keep thanking God," and whatever else I could think of to stay in His good graces and keep the streak alive. I was so close to the round of my life, and I didn't want to do or stop doing anything that would jeopardize my score. Here too, I was getting cocky in my conversations with God. I was thinking that if I played the humility card and pledged my undying support for God, He would have no other choice but to complete the miracle round for me.

I had often wondered what the Apostle Peter felt like the night the Romans arrested Jesus in the Garden of Gethsemane, when in less than one hour he fulfilled a prophecy that Jesus had given him earlier that evening. After the Lord's Supper, as Jesus was preparing them for the events that would follow, He had this exchange with the apostles:

"This very night you will all fall away on account of me, for it is written:

'I will strike the shepherd,
  and the sheep of the flock will be scattered.'

But after I have risen, I will go ahead of you into Galilee."

Peter replied, "Even if all fall away on account of you, I never will."

"Truly I tell you," Jesus answered, "this very night, before the rooster crows, you will disown me three times."

But Peter declared, "Even if I have to die with you, I will never disown you." And all the other disciples said the same. (Matthew 26:31–35)

And, just as Jesus had predicted, as the night wore on, Peter denied knowing Him, not once, not twice, but three times, with the third denial followed by the sound of the town rooster's crow. Talk about cutting straight to the heart! At that moment, Peter knew what he had done, despite his insistence that it would never happen.

At the completion of my "miracle" golf round, I had a pretty good idea of how Peter felt that night. My transgression paled compared to his, but it came from the same place of arrogance and pride in my abilities. I am not referring to my athletic abilities, mind you, but my ability to control my emotions and my ability to make good on guarantees that I had no business making. What had I guaranteed God? That no matter what might happen the rest of the way, I would not stop praising Him for the awesome day that I was having. In effect, I had laid down a challenge to God and said: "Go ahead, throw anything you want at me, I can handle it. I am master of my emotions, and nothing that you can do will trip me up!"

On the fifteenth hole, the most difficult one on the course, I hit two of the longest and straightest back-to-back shots I have ever hit in my life. This was more proof to me that God was rewarding my incredible faith. Four shots later, I was shaking my head, wondering how I could get the ball to go 450 yards in just two shots but take four shots for the last twenty-five feet. I felt a twinge of frustration at that point, but I was still thankful for what I had experienced so far.

Walking towards the next hole, I did a mental recalculation of my possible final score and realized that it still would represent my best round ever. Again, I offered another silent prayer to God, along with a steely resolve to refocus my thoughts and get back to my game.

It's interesting how important the number three is. We all have heard and probably used the phrase "Third time's a charm!" many times in our lives. It takes three attempts for us to get something right. There are lots of passages in the Bible where the number three figures prominently. As we just saw, Peter denied knowing Jesus three times after His arrest. After Jesus had risen and was visiting with the apostles, He asked Peter three times, "Peter, do you love me?" (John 21:15–17).

Why did Jesus do this? I think it was His way of telling Peter, "Hey man, slow down and think about what I'm asking you. Remember what happened the last time you were so sure of yourself?" When Jesus challenged him again, Peter got a little angry but began to briefly reflect on his response. Asked a third time, I think that Peter was humbled by the memory of his three denials.

Now, I was staring down the last three holes of the day! I still believed at that point that I was in control of my emotions and that I would somehow pull it off. God used those last three holes for what I'll simply call a "teaching opportunity." I had spent the whole day believing that the creator of the universe was walking down the fairway with me. When I finished that day, I knew for sure. As I played those last three holes of golf, each successive shot got uglier and uglier until, on the third shot of the final three holes, I hurled my club across the fairway and cursed from the depths of my bowels, "GOD DAMNIT!"

Had I been a character in a movie, the next sound you would have heard would have been the shrill crow of a rooster. Except that it wasn't a movie; it was the middle of the afternoon, and I doubt that there was a rooster within ten miles of the golf course. But at that very moment, my heart was pierced in much the same way that Peter's was when he heard the rooster that would signal his downfall, or "falling away," as Jesus termed it. I was convicted by the awareness that my attempts to assure the Lord my allegiance would never falter were just as empty as Peter's promise that he would never deny Jesus.

And then, just as quickly as the shame and remorse came over me, God washed it away. God washes away our sins when we come to him in genuine humility and repentance. I finished the round with an 80 on my scorecard, probably one of the top ten rounds I've ever recorded. But the story I had to tell after that round, with its disappointing finish, far outweighed the story I would have had to share had I simply finished out the round of golf as I had started it, with near perfection.

Did God speak to me that day? I know He did! He spoke to me through the beauty of His creation and the splendor of the warm sun and the vibrant colors of the green grass. He spoke to me through the blessings that He gave me for the first fourteen and a half holes. God spoke to me through the fellowship and encouragement of the three guys who got to share in my experience that day. He also spoke to me in answering the challenge that I had laid at His feet as I approached the last three holes. The Holy Spirit convicted me of how I had failed in my vain promise. Finally, I heard His voice that day through the grace that says, "You failed your promise, but I'm giving you another chance, because you are my son and I love you."

I hope that one of these days I will play a full eighteen holes with the near perfection that I got to experience for most of that memorable day. I have tried to recreate it by repeating all the things that I did that day, but my suspicion is that it was a one-of-a-kind gift that God had for me that day. God doesn't have a formula for how He communicates with us. He does it on His terms, in His timing, for His purposes, and to tell us what we need to hear. Sometimes God's message to us can be understood in the blink of an eye, or maybe in a four-hour round of golf—but sometimes it takes much longer!

CHAPTER 15

HOW DID THE PREACHER KNOW?

[11]"so is my word that goes out from my mouth: It will not return to me empty, but will accomplish what I desire and achieve the purpose for which I sent it." (ISAIAH 55:11 NIV)

I f you attend a place of worship regularly, it's inevitable that one day this will happen to you. You'll be sitting in the crowd when the pastor, priest, rabbi, imam, shaman, or whatever they are called in your place of worship will say something that stops you in your tracks. You'll pull out of your slouch and become fixated on what, until that moment, could just as well have been *blah, blah, blah*.

The person up front just woke you from your slumber, laying out a line that cuts right into your heart. Maybe it's about how we need to "love our neighbors as ourselves," and just that morning you wondered for the hundredth time what is stopping you from saying hello to the neighbor next door, the neighbor whom you know, through the grapevine, is going through a painful divorce.

Maybe the words that got you to divert your wandering eyes off the young blond in the too-tight blouse was something like: "Anyone who looks at a woman lustfully has already committed adultery with her in his heart." Maybe that starts you thinking about how your "occasional" visits to internet porn sites are spiraling out of control, and that if your wife ever finds out, she will leave you. But you just can't stop.

Whatever the words are that get you to sit up and pay attention, they have that effect because they speak to something that you are experiencing, something that you are struggling with, something that you fear right now, right where you sit. It's as if you had spilled your guts last week on one of the "Get to Know You" cards that they put in the church bulletin, and then the pastor dedicated this week's sermon to you and your dirty little secret.

The only problem is that you didn't fill out one of those cards last week. In fact, you have never filled out one of those cards at all, and even if you had, you would never have shared *that*! And so, the internal dialogue starts in your head: *How could the guy up on stage possibly know what I am going through right now? Did someone tell him about my struggles? Why on this day of all days did he pick to call me out personally on my addiction to pornography when just this morning I narrowly escaped being found out by my wife?*

The skeptic will say that this is pure coincidence and is bound to happen, because the same general themes get dealt with repeatedly in churches. The longer someone attends there, the reasoning goes, the greater the likelihood is that the message will hit upon something that is going on in their life. There is a degree of truth to that thought. I suspect that most churches have a repertoire of lessons and teachings that they cycle through every year. The church I have now been at for over twenty years fits that mold. So then, it's just a matter of time before the week's lesson will line up with something that you are struggling with, right?

I don't think the skeptic should get off so easily here, however. How do they explain the guy who is not a regular church attendee but walks into a church and, within minutes, feels like the pastor is speaking to him and him alone?

For years, I had tried to get my younger brother David to come to church with me during one of his family's annual summer treks to California. Dave lived in Seattle with his wife Shannon and their three young children. Each year, they would plan a vacation that would have them spending the better part of a week visiting friends and family in our area. They usually stayed at my house. With each visit, I would invite him to come to church with us. Invariably, he would respond with a polite "We'll see."

One summer, Dave finally gave in. In some ways, he had no choice, because the excuses he used in the past— "It's not fair to leave Shannon with the kids" or "I promised the kids I would take them to the beach on Sunday"—weren't available to him then. Dave was by himself this time, making an unexpected visit that happily coincided with my fiftieth birthday party; it was unexpected because he and his family had just been to California a couple of weeks prior.

Much as I'd like to say that Dave came to help his big brother celebrate a milestone birthday, the truth was that his wife had bought him a one-way ticket with the suggestion that he take as much time as he needed. Dave had been traveling a tough road for some years, and things just kept getting worse. It wasn't enough that he and his wife were growing farther and farther apart. Right in the middle of all the marital strife, David had gotten a diagnosis of Stage IV esophageal cancer. His first doctors had read this diagnosis like it was a death sentence. In a testament to his powerful will, or maybe his Irish ancestry (you've heard the term "hard-headed Irishman"), Dave fought and won the battle against a diagnosis that came with only a 3 percent survival rate. The battle to save his marriage had not been faring as well, unfortunately.

I'd learned over the years not to set my expectations too high about the likelihood that Dave would say yes to my invitation, but each time he visited, I would extend one. And so, with all the possible "outs" stripped away, this time he said yes! I knew it wasn't out of a sense of guilt over having declined my invitation for so many years; nor was he simply thinking, "Oh crap, you finally caught me with no plausible excuse." I could see in his eyes and sense in my heart the brokenness that he was feeling. This was the kind of brokenness that God uses to get our attention. I knew it well myself.

And then my doubting mind commenced its usual gyrations. I worried if things would be just right for Dave's visit. Who would teach this week? What would the lesson be? Would it apply to Dave and what he was going through right now? Who would lead worship? Would the songs be ones that would speak to Dave like they did to me? Would we run into any of the men I know who had been praying for Dave for years, and who would give him a warm welcome?

It was as if by worrying about it, I could make things just right. My small brain had this delusion that having control over all the variables would also mean that I could ensure the outcome that I desperately wanted: for Dave to hear the voice of a loving God who knew where he was and knew what he was going through. I wanted Dave to listen to the voice of a loving Father who just wanted to hold him in His arms and speak into his heart, not to chastise him for making a mess of his marriage, or for not being the perfect husband, or for not being the perfect father, but to let him know that through all this He was walking through the pain with Dave. In reality, of course, I wasn't in control of anything more than just turning on the ignition, driving to church, parking the car, and walking into the worship center with my brother by my side.

It's funny how much we want to play God, isn't it? We are seem-ingly intelligent human beings walking around with this crazy notion that somehow, we have ultimate control not only of ourselves but of the world as a whole. The Bible would call this pride, or arrogance. In my case, it's perhaps best called stupidity. In my deepest parts, I know I am not in control. Like most people who wander the earth, I struggle with my self-esteem daily. And yet there is still this part of me that continues to cling to the idea that my involvement (or lack thereof) in anything is the key to the success (or failure) of that thing.

I can remember as a kid thinking that my favorite team would have won, if only I had been watching the game or listening to the radio instead of playing catch with a friend! This was the crazy thinking of a seven-year-old kid (although, to my credit, there is a scientific theory called the "butterfly effect," which posits that a small action, like the flapping of a butterfly's wings in China, can set off a chain of events that end with a tornado in Oklahoma). It is normal for young children to have a very self-centered view of the world. That is why a young child will often blame themselves when something bad happens in their family. To a five or six-year-old boy, the thinking often goes: "If only I had been a good little boy, mommy and daddy would not have gotten a divorce."

But how does that kind of thinking continue with a guy well into his adulthood? My guess is that it probably stems from some early childhood trauma that left me stuck in the part of childhood where kids believe that the world revolves around them. One thing I do know now that I did not know then, however, is that God speaks to us even in our self-centeredness.

Dave and I arrived at church a few minutes past the scheduled start time. My wife, sensing his fragile state, thought it best to let us go on our own that day. I got stressed immediately, convinced as I was that if Dave missed anything, the expedition wouldn't be a success, and he'd be eternally doomed to the nightmare he'd been living, with no hope of escape. The only problem with such reasoning is that God is way bigger than my weak faith can even comprehend. After all, He parted the Red Sea long enough for millions of Israelites to escape the oncoming Egyptian hordes. And mind you, they were all on foot. Given that, one would think that God should be able to operate in the slightly more friendly environs of an evangelical Christian church in modern-day America, where chariots and rampaging warriors are not part of the landscape.

As we found seats in the already crowded worship center, I resigned myself to the reality that I had done my part in getting Dave inside the church. Now, my job was to shut up and let God work. And work He did. Of course, I was still going to continue worrying about every little detail and nuance of the service. Would the worship songs speak to what David was going through right now? Would this week's teaching have a direct application to the burdens that he was carrying? Would Dave be paying attention at just the right moments?

And so, we sang and we listened, and we sang some more and then listened some more. I kept looking over at my brother, wondering how much he was picking up, how much he was being affected by the music, by the teaching, by the experience. As I sat there calculating which of the distinct concepts being taught would collide with his condition and finally pierce his heart, I had to resist the temptation to lean into Dave every few minutes and whisper, "Did you hear what he just said?"

The funny thing is that we are but bit players in the story of God's pursuit of any individual's heart. Time and time again, though, we rather naively cast ourselves as the star of the show. It's not that we are unimportant to the production, because we do play a part. We might even walk away with the Best Supporting Actor/Actress occasionally, but it is God's show. He is the writer, director, producer, casting agent, and of course, the star.

Dave's tears that morning told me that God had once again put on an award-winning performance, working in my brother's ears and in his heart. As we stood in silence, arms wrapped around each other and tears flowing, no words were necessary. Certainly not mine, for they would only have cheapened what my brother was experiencing then. The creator of the universe knew who Dave was, knew his pain, and loved him right where he stood. Through all the pain, the fear, the broken dreams, and the uncertainty of what the future might hold, there was hope. And hope does not disappoint.

As the service ended and we made our way towards the aisle, my brother motioned to the altar, where the pastor was conversing with a small group of people. With all the sincerity in the world, he asked, "Did you call the pastor last night and tell him what I have been going through, because he was speaking right to my heart?"

I could only smile.

CHAPTER 16

THE ANSWER IS BLOWING IN THE WIND

²"Do not conform any longer to the pattern of this world, but be transformed by the renewing of your mind. Then you will be able to test and approve what God's will is—his good, pleasing and perfect will." (ROMANS 12:2 NIV)

will freely admit that I struggle with the Bible. To be clear, I am not talking about the content of the Bible, or the idea that it is the inspired word of God. I don't struggle with what some people would call discrepancies or contradictions. And I don't struggle with the many stories that suggest to some that God is a vengeful old man, full of wrath, waiting to rain death and destruction down on men, women, and children (Okay, maybe I struggle with those just a little).

What I truly struggle with is opening the Bible and reading it regularly. Why? Because it's easier to surf the web, or maybe because the TV remote fits nicely in my hands when I am sitting comfortably in the easy chair. Really, though, what holds me back the most is intellectual laziness. It is hard work figuring out what the author of a passage of Scripture is trying to say, or how the passage applies to my life. And there is a part of me that doesn't want my faith journey to be hard work.

The other component of my struggle with opening my Bible regularly is that there is a part of me that says, "Yeah, I get it already. I don't need to read what I already know." And maybe that is the real problem. A small smug voice inside my head continually overpowers what I know in my heart to be true: that my grasp of the Bible is akin to a one-year-old child's understanding of the alphabet. And yet if I open my Bible right now, I will notice that there is an awful lot of underlining and highlighting, which makes me wonder, when did I read all this?

Several years ago, I was at our church's annual men's retreat, which takes place in the early fall at one of the many Christian camps and retreat centers tucked away in the coastal mountain range near Santa Cruz. "Man Camp," as we sometimes refer to it, is a weekend when the men of the church withdraw from the routines of their everyday lives and try to be spiritual for a few days.

Let's face it: most guys have a really hard time being spiritual. It's not that they don't want to be, it's just that the society we live in today looks at spirituality with some disdain, as if it were a sign of weakness. Most guys just limp through life wearing their masks and stuffing all their junk inside, all the while giving off the air that their lives are totally together, and they have it all figured out. Only they don't— or, I should say, WE don't.

The men's retreat gives guys the opportunity, if only for a weekend, to get away from all this, to explore the spirituality inside each one of them that is bursting to see the light of day. Once each year, one hundred or more guys—some of them reluctantly, some at the insistence of their wives, and some quite eagerly—head up the hill to get their annual spiritual fix.

The weekend isn't purely spiritual. We set aside a good portion of Saturday for activities like mountain biking, hiking, paintball, golf, and a variety of team sports. It allows guys to flex their muscles, sweat, and try to prove their athletic prowess to the rest of the guys and themselves. Guys like to do that, don't they? They like to prove that the glory days are not yet over by overexerting themselves in front of a bunch of other guys who are doing the same thing. I always thought it would be a splendid idea to have a chiropractor on-site. I know they would keep busy!

There is always some tension each year when the men's leadership team, which I am a part of, gets together to plan the upcoming retreat. Some of us believe that a retreat should be a departure from what guys do the other fifty-one weekends of the year. But some think that if we do not pack the event with opportunities for guys to do some of what they usually do on the weekends, then they probably will just stay at home. I mean, seriously, who *would* want to trade in the comfort of a warm bed for a hard plywood bunk in a dormitory setting? Surely, your cabin will have at least one guy who goes to bed each night outfitted in a Darth Vader-like CPAP mask, while the surrounding guys all swear that *they* don't snore. Where do I sign up for *that*?

Of course, anyone who attends a church retreat knows that there will be at least *some* spiritual stuff during the weekend. You would kind of expect that, right? Besides, most of the guys that take the plunge are secretly yearning for a little of what they can't get from their work softball league or regular Saturday golf game.

The weekend usually starts with some teaching on Friday evening, followed by small group gatherings, or "cabin time," where we challenge everyone to be vulnerable and share with each other. It's called being transparent, and it is something that most men find extremely hard to do! After a hearty breakfast, the Saturday schedule looks like this: morning teaching session, outdoor activities, dinner, and then the evening talk. The centerpiece of the weekend is a campfire that goes well into the night. Another chance to be transparent! In a nutshell, the retreat is an opportunity to do lots of things with lots of guys, most of whom were strangers before Friday night. Sounds different from a typical weekend, doesn't it?

One year, the team decided we would try to slow things down and push the spiritual envelope a little more. We would get the guys to spend some time alone. We would set aside time when they could meditate, read their Bibles, and perhaps be still long enough to hear from God. We arranged the schedule so that after the morning teaching, and before the outdoor activities, there would be quiet time. We challenged the guys to grab their Bibles and find a place somewhere on the property where they could meditate on the lesson and spend some time in Scripture. They would then come back and share what God had placed in their hearts.

As a member of the organizing team each year, I usually spend a good deal of my time at the retreat simply making sure that everything runs smoothly and that everyone has a good time. Mind you, those are not things that the team asks me to do, but I do them because of the blessings that I have received from the retreat over the years. I want all the other men to have some of those experiences. I end up missing good portions of the weekend because I'm running around like a fussy mother at her daughter's wedding reception. But this year, if I wanted to be an exemplary model for the men, I knew I would need to resist the urge to intervene.

After the morning's teaching was over, we gave the guys their instructions and unleashed them in the woods. I, too, headed out, Bible tucked squarely under my arm, to find a place of quiet solitude. I knew that if I stayed too close to the center of camp, I would surely be tempted to check on things and maybe even to break up small groups of guys who were terrified of being alone. That would all be at the expense of my own quiet time.

After walking for maybe ten minutes, I fixed my eyes on a fallen tree that looked like it would be a comfortable spot to rest and begin the exercise. The trouble was that in my state of perpetual agitation, I wasn't sure if finding "time alone with God" was even attainable. I had already spent most of the morning's teaching time checking on details and surveying the room to make sure that everyone was focusing on the speaker and getting maximum value out of the teaching. I somehow had this notion that my vigilance was essential for a room full of men to connect with the speaker and their message. When will I ever learn?

Easing into a comfortable nook in the fallen tree, I opened my Bible with no inkling of what to focus on or where in the multitude of pages to start. After a quick prayer asking God to calm my mind and give me a signal of what He wanted me to hear during our alone time, I opened to the book of Galatians. My reason for picking this book was simple: I had never actually read it before and thus was sure that *this* was where I would find the pearls of wisdom God wanted me to take from our time together.

Satisfied with my logic and understanding of how God works, I scanned the words on the page. I use the word "scan" because what I was doing could only loosely be defined as reading. After getting through the first chapter, I tried to contemplate the meaning of what I had just read. Gazing up at the towering eucalyptus trees with a smug sense of accomplishment, I awaited the wave that would wash over me and fill me with newfound wisdom. I got nothing, although I am sure that God was silently smiling at the scene.

Perhaps I had raced through the passage too quickly? Maybe I wasn't concentrating hard enough? Were the chirping of the birds and the raw beauty of the wilderness around me getting in the way? I was seeing the words and vaguely understanding what the writer was saying, but no bells or sirens were ringing in my head or heart, as I was sure should be happening. I was spending time alone with the creator of the universe, wasn't I? He is the author of earthquakes and tsunamis, and He can create quite a racket when He wants to. Surely, there should have been some external commotion to signal He was speaking. But I got nothing. A quick glance at my watch showed I still had twenty minutes. There was no way I was going back to the gathering with nothing to share. What kind of role model would I be?

In my infinite wisdom, I decided that maybe God had not arrived yet, that maybe He needed an opportunity to catch up with me. At this point, my pea-sized brain kicked into gear and suggested that I read Galatians again … only slower this time.

So, I navigated back to the beginning of the book and went through the motions again. Within seconds, I was distracted by the sound of the wind rustling in the trees. When I looked back down to focus on my reading, a sudden gust of wind caught the pages of the book and flipped them backwards to the middle of a book called Corinthians. There, my eyes settled on a particular paragraph. It wasn't the passage I was supposed to be reading, though, so I thumbed my way back to Galatians and readjusted my grip to minimize the effects of the now-irritating breeze.

With even greater determination, I returned to the original passage, reading it for the third time. Almost as if on cue, another small gust of wind grabbed the razor-thin pages and flipped them back not merely to Corinthians, but to the *exact same* spot as before. Again, my eyes were pulled to the passage I had just chosen not to read. By now, I was getting angry … but about what? Was I mad at the wind? Or at my weak grip? Or was I a little angry with God for not letting me have my time of inspiration?

Still believing that I was in charge, I did my best to clear my mind of the negative feelings that were dominating me. I took a deep breath and turned back to my target reading in Galatians. The instant I took my hands off the pages to reposition my grip on the spine, a gentle breeze once again lifted the pages back to the same place, the same paragraph I had avoided twice before.

Normally, my instinct would have been to slam the book shut and fling it as far as possible, with expletives streaming from my lips. But that didn't happen. Instead, I gently closed the book over my thumb to save the spot where the wind had continually returned me to. And I smiled. Then I laughed. And then I reopened the book and read. God had finally gotten my attention. It took three tries, but He got my attention. And that's not to knock His attempts, but rather to admit that it took *me* three tries to understand what He was trying to say to me: "I have something very specific that I want you to read, and I'll show you exactly where it is!" My proud and stubborn nature had revealed once again that, "The third time is a charm" and God had used it to perfection!

When something unexpected assaults our consciousness, we immediately dismiss it with some form of "No, that can't be true, or I would have figured it out earlier." As the second wave of the attack mounts, we retreat to our previous assertion, but with a more cautious "Nah, that can't be right.... or can it?" And finally, as the truth of the matter hits us once again, we succumb, throw our hands up, and exclaim, "Okay, I guess that's right!" We might try to build ourselves up with the thought that we were just employing healthy skepticism—but we know we've been humbled. We may then feel the kind of shame that says, "You should have known better. You're better than that!" And that is if we can even show ourselves a bit of kindness. What was more often the case with me as a younger person (although it still slips out sometimes) is that I would berate myself for not knowing. "You should have known" became "You idiot, you are such a loser, you should have known that."

What I know through experience is that when God infuses us with humility—through a life lesson or some undeserved blessing—he does so without sticking a knife in our sides and gleefully twisting it for the maximum "I told you so!" effect. It is a humility meted out and grounded in love. God's love says, "You have so much to learn, my son, and I want to teach it you, and it won't offend me if you ignore my advances."

On that day at the men's retreat, the third time was the charm, for sure! When I finally read the passage, it filled me with a sense of awe and wonder at what God had just put before me. It spoke to my heart, to my condition, and it left me with a renewed sense that even though I am a tiny speck in the universe, the creator of it all cares about me. He is a Father that is intimately involved in and interested in every aspect of my life.

Here's the funny thing, though. Today, five years later, I don't even remember what the passage was that God's voice, through the gentle

breeze, directed me to. I know it was in one of the two books of
Corinthians in the New Testament, but as for which chapter, verses,
and message ... I have no clue. I do remember that the passage spoke
to me in such an overwhelming and convincing manner that I knew,
in my heart, that God had taken time out of his busy day to talk to
me. And that's all that matters!

In the Old Testament, there is a story where the prophet Elijah, fearing for his life, embarks on a forty-day journey through the desert.
Assisted by angels along the way, he comes to a place called Horeb,
which means "the mountain of God," and he rests there for the night.
Upon waking up the next morning, Elijah hears the voice of God.
After a short back-and-forth in which God asks Elijah why he is there
hiding at Horeb, God tells Elijah: "Go out and stand on the mountain in the presence of the LORD, for the LORD is about to pass
by" (1 Kings 19:11). The rest of the passage continues: "Then a great
and powerful wind tore the mountains apart and shattered the rocks
before the LORD, but the LORD was not in the wind. After the
wind there was an earthquake, but the LORD was not in the earthquake. After the earthquake came a fire, but the LORD was not in
the fire. And after the fire came a gentle whisper. When Elijah heard
it [the whisper], he pulled his cloak over his face and went out and
stood at the mouth of the cave" (1 Kings 19:11–13).

Not gale-force winds, not an earthquake, not even a flash fire—none
of those things were enough to dislodge Elijah from his hiding place.
What finally gave him the courage to move from his spot was the gentle
whisper of God in his ear. Most of us do not differ from Elijah, do we?
How often do we look for fireworks and a marching band as a signal that
maybe, just maybe, God is trying to get our attention? We do so instead
of listening to the gentle whispers in our ear, or the stirrings in our heart.

It's so easy to ignore the voice in our head that says, "That guy looks like he needs help. Why don't you give him some money?" Just as quickly as the thought comes, we can be assaulted with a string of counterarguments and intellectual rationalizations that often result in us just passing on by with our hands stuck in our pockets. Our rational side argues that they would surely use any money for drugs or alcohol; that is not what God would want, therefore the voice must not have been His. Our thinking continues that if God had really wanted us to help this stranger, He would have made it crystal clear: maybe a rainbow encircling the man's head or perhaps a quick trumpet blast from the heavenly realms? And so, we just walk on by, smugly satisfied that our powers of spiritual discernment have once again proven infallible. And, at that point, God smiles and shakes His head.

Undoubtedly, from time to time, God needs to use a loud bang—or, as I like to describe it, a two-by-four upside the head—to get our attention. Sometimes He needs to use an earthquake, tsunami, or hurricane to get us to drop our iPads and smartphones, close our laptops, and sit up and pay attention. But if we are honest with ourselves, we should be able to admit that the only reason that God needs to use drastic measures to get our attention is that most of the time we are just not listening. And, even if we are listening, we may have a hard time believing that it is God's voice we are hearing.

But often, God's voice is a gentle breeze, turning the page to where we need to be.

CHAPTER 17

HIS PLAN OR YOUR PLAN?

[3] The tempter came to him and said, "If you are the Son of God, tell these stones to become bread." [4] Jesus answered, "It is written: 'Man shall not live on bread alone, but on every word that comes from the mouth of God.'" (MATTHEW 4:3-4 NIV)

A few years ago, I received an email from my good friend Dave Larson. Dave was the care pastor at our church. His email stated that he had spoken with a younger man named Rick (another Rick!) who had placed a communication card in the Sunday offering bucket. The card contained a request to enter into a mentoring relationship with an older man from the church. In Dave's email, he simply asked if I knew of anyone who might fit the bill and be interested in mentoring a younger man who was looking to become "unstuck" in his spiritual life.

After thinking about all the different men who I knew from church, my initial response was, "I can't think of anyone offhand, but let me get back with you." One thought that had crossed my mind at the time was whether *I* might be a worthy candidate for this role. I was already something of a mentor to some other men I had met over the years. Yet a voice in my head told me that none of these were "official" mentoring relationships, so I quickly eliminated myself from the pool of eligible men to mentor Rick.

What is it that makes us think this kind of relationship—an older man mentoring a younger man, or any kind of relationship, for that matter—needs to be official? What does that mean, anyway? Do we need some certification or degree to befriend another person and help them through tough times? I guess if those tough times involve a major illness, medical or psychological, and our help would constitute practicing medicine or providing psychiatric care, then some sort of certificate or license would be in order. But I knew that mentoring does not involve prescribing drugs or performing surgery—or at least it shouldn't! So why did I feel like I needed an official blessing? Maybe it was just a rationalization due to fear of the unknown. Accepting an assignment to mentor someone I had never met sounded daunting.

Interestingly, Dave had copied the email to one other person, Scott, who is a church elder and a colleague of mine on the men's leadership team at our church. Scott suggested an older gentleman that he thought might be interested in taking on this role. Without going into details, Dave responded that he didn't feel like this candidate was right for the assignment. A couple of weeks went by with no further communication from Dave on the subject, and I honestly had not given it much more thought. Part of me just assumed that Dave had, through other circles, found someone to help Rick.

While cleaning out my email inbox one night, my eyes settled on the two or three emails that had passed back and forth between Dave and me. Something compelled me to open and reread the string of emails. As it turned out, I had never actually heard from Dave saying that he had found a suitable mentor for Rick. With just a hint of guilt gnawing at me, I crafted an email to Dave saying I was curious if he had found someone. I hoped that his response would be something like, "Thanks, it's all taken care of!" But something in my heart told me it was not the case. I offered that, if Rick were still looking, I would volunteer to get together with him for an initial meeting. My thought was that it would quickly be clear that I was probably not the right guy, but I could at least say that I had done my due diligence.

I got an almost immediate response from Dave saying that he had not yet found anyone to meet with Rick and thanking me for volunteering. The message included Rick's email address, cell number, and the exhortation to call him and "see where it goes!" Oh boy, what had I gotten myself into now? There was this part of me that just assumed Dave would see through the smokescreen and suggest that we keep looking for a more appropriate person to take on this mentor role. Maybe some guy who was older, wiser, more mature, more grounded in his spiritual life. Some guy who was doing all the right things in his walk with God and had mastered the "spiritual disciplines." Someone who actually had his shit together! Of course, I could have just cited a conflict or pulled the old "I'm just too busy right now for another commitment" card. Instead, I called Rick.

What I have come to understand over the years is that, if we had any clue of what God's plans for us looked like, any inkling of what the future might hold, we would run and hide. It wouldn't be the ultimate destination that would be so scary for us; it would be the journey along the way.

I'd like to propose a hypothetical scenario. Let's say you are an exceptional high school athlete, a football player. Not only that, but you are also a straight-A student who is involved in student government and respected by everyone in the school, students, and faculty alike. You are also actively involved in your church youth group and a frequent participant in a couple of service organizations in the local community. You have it all together.

One day, God decides He is going to share with you the plans He has for your life. You come home from football practice, and there is something in the mailbox addressed to you. By the size and shape of the package, you guess that it's a CD or DVD. You scan the front of the package to see if there are any clues as to the contents. You see your name and address, then turn your attention to the top left corner, where you see an ornate address label with one word on it: "GOD." Down in the bottom left corner is a little message scrawled with a black Sharpie that says, "My plans for your life." Figuring that this is a joke your teammates have put together, you drop your gear and head up to your room and pop in the DVD.

The DVD starts out with a time-lapse sequence of the sun rising and setting over the ocean. The background music sounds like angels playing harps. As the ocean scene slowly fades to black, you see white block-letter words scrolling from the top of the screen—like how the *Star Wars* movies start, "In a galaxy far, far away…" You are a little puzzled but just think, "Wow, those guys did a good job on this video!" Yet as the words scroll down the screen, it hits you that this just might not be the doing of your buddies, who are too stupid or lazy to pull something like this off. But if not them, then who?

Suddenly, you notice a barely audible voice, which gets louder as the words fade from the screen. The voice is peaceful, and something about it tells you that you may want to pay attention. The voice, now fully audible, pauses as if to give you time to pull in your chair and straighten up.

And then it begins: "My cherished son, I have chosen you out of all the people in the world to get a glimpse of the plans that I have for your life, something that I have never done before and will never do again."

There is a long pause, and you edge closer to the screen.

"In this video, I have laid out the next fifty years of your life in reverse order. The beginning will show you at the pinnacle of your career in football as the winning coach of Super Bowl XCV (in the year 2061) and proceed backward through your life, showing you how you got there. At the end of the video, you may accept or reject this life I have chosen for you. Regardless of your choice, you will have no memory of your decision, or of this video. When you are ready, click on the 'Here's Your Life' button on the screen to start the show."

As the voice fades out, the white block-letter words roll down the screen and stop when the screen fills with the following Bible verse: "For I know the plans I have for you … plans to prosper you and not to harm you … " (Jeremiah 29:11).

Let's say that what you have seen and heard so far, has not scared the hell out of you, but rather has left you intrigued. You move closer, adjust the volume on your computer, take a deep breath, and click on the button to start the show.

Just as promised, the video opens with a scene that you have watched unfold on television many, many times, the hoisting of the ceremonial Gatorade container over the head of the unsuspecting coach who is watching the scoreboard as it counts down to zero in anticipation of the pandemonium that soon will unfold. You lean in to focus on the coach who, while sporting an all-white mustache and beard and a paunch that reveals years of not so healthy living, looks suspiciously like you. Or at least what you imagine you could look like in fifty years. There before your eyes, in full HD, you see yourself in a scene that not even Hollywood could have staged. You are the winning coach celebrating your first Super Bowl victory!

As the video unfolds (remember that it is in reverse chronological order), you count backward through the myriad of experiences, events, and relationships that have brought you to this pinnacle of success. You see yourself as a sought-after speaker addressing large groups of inner-city youth with a message about how God has worked in your life and brought you through adversity to become a winning football coach. There is the scene of you marrying your high school sweetheart, and later raising children.

But you also see: years of toil and frustration as an assistant coach who is passed over for so many years until your first big break. The ten-plus years you played in the NFL, bouncing around from team to team, never quite fitting in with the coach or system. The career-ending knee injury that befell you right in the middle of the season your team went to the Super Bowl. You witness the multitude of less severe injuries over the years that kept you off the field for measurable parts of every season, and for which there are painful reminders every time you get in or out of bed or climb a flight of stairs. You also see yourself getting pulled into the party life of a high-profile professional athlete and becoming addicted to cocaine and other dubious recreational pursuits, all of which ends in an ugly and painful divorce from that sweetheart, who just couldn't take it anymore. Wow, is this getting depressing or what?

But it isn't all bad. You get to see yourself standing up on the podium as the commissioner of the NFL reads your name as the seventh player taken in the draft, the first draft pick of the San Francisco 49ers. You watch as, with your college sweetheart wife looking on, you sign a multimillion-dollar contract, which includes a signing bonus that is large enough to make most people set for life. There you are, the star running back of a large college football powerhouse, prancing into the end zone to put the finishing touches on a perfect season and a shot at the national championship. And then, just as quickly, the scene changes to an athletic trainer injecting you with steroids, which will give you the extra edge you need to compete. And on and on it goes, back to your present. There is victory and defeat, joy and pain, ecstasy and agony. And then the video ends.

And now, as promised at the start of the video, you have a choice: accept this path that God has planned and drawn out for you, or decline and choose a path of your own. Do the glory and admiration outweigh the pain, heartache, blood, sweat, and tears that were necessary to get you to that point of fulfillment? Do they also outweigh the poor life decisions you made along the way?

Now, I'm not a betting man (okay, I do like to play a little poker), but I would venture to say you not only will hit the Decline button on the screen, but the next move will be to turn in your uniform and walk away from the game forever. If we are totally honest with ourselves, we would all say no to the above offer. Who among us would sign up in advance for all the trials and tribulations? Who would say yes to the pain and agony, the disappointments and setbacks, that are guaranteed to occur in each of our lives?

Most of us approach life with this absurd notion that, if we can just accumulate enough education, money, influence, power, etc., we will sidestep most, if not all, of the pitfalls and roadblocks that present themselves during our lifetimes. I wonder where we got that idea?

Fortunately, the preceding vignette is something that could only happen in a movie or a novel. God loves us too much to put that kind of pressure on us. Again, He knows that if we could see the full journey before starting the trip, we would all turn and run ... every single one of us. And God should know. It's called human nature, and He created it.

So, back to me and Rick. I faced a decision: to decline an assignment that I was not sure I could handle, or to step out in faith and trust the many promises that God has made to us. When we put our confidence in God, He will always be there to walk through it with us. I ultimately chose the "step out in faith" option. Looking back now, I wonder why I ever doubted my suitability for the assignment. Once again, God revealed to me over time that HIS plan is always a lot better than what I can come up with on my own.

Rick and I hit it off right from the start and agreed to meet every Monday morning. What unfolded over the next few months was something that I have seen happen time and time again when I have humbled myself to God's promptings and moved forward despite my fears. God's plan was a two-way relationship all along, and not the one-way mentor-to-mentee relationship that I had pictured in my mind. After the first meeting, during which I gave Rick a couple of readings and memorization exercises to help get him "unstuck," the relationship quickly developed into one in which I was receiving just as much mentoring as I was dishing out. Rick, who is almost twenty years my junior, had life experiences, perspectives on faith, and a heart that God knew I needed to tap into to help me with my own struggles. And so, we both helped each other become "unstuck."

Right after the New Year, Rick presented me with an envelope as we were wrapping up our Monday morning meeting. He said he had written me a letter, but he wanted to explain what was in the letter before I read it. Rick reflected on one of our first meetings during which I had shared with him my desire to enroll in a local seminary to pursue a master's degree in marriage and family therapy and work towards becoming a therapist. I had explained to him that much of the ministry work I had been doing at church felt like counseling already. But the biggest motivator was a sense that God seemed to be calling me in that direction.

Rick knew that the only thing holding me back was the financial commitment. My oldest daughter Kellie was just finishing college, my son Thomas was in the middle of it, and my youngest daughter was just a couple of years away from it. Making the financial commitment that graduate school involves did not seem like a wise move. Maybe I was a little gun-shy given my experience with the smoothie business!

Rick then reminded me of a conversation months earlier in which he had shared with me his financial situation, which involved an annual payment from his father's estate. The annual check, while not enough to make him rich, provided him and his wife Ashley with some degree of financial security. He had explained how it was their heart's desire not to just spend the money on themselves, but to use the money in ways pleasing to God. Rick shared how, after one of our meetings, he had felt God was convicting him to help me with my financial need. Even though his wife had given her blessing to the idea, though, he had not moved forward.

And then Rick dropped the bomb on me that inevitably brought me to tears. He reminded me of our last meeting before the holidays and recounted how, after hearing about an ongoing struggle he and Ashley had been dealing with, I had given some advice and encouragement that, in his words, "blew me out of the water!" I had provided a perspective he had never considered. Rick then told me I had been more helpful in that single interchange than any counselor he had ever gone to in the past. He thought I would make an excellent counselor and wanted to help me get started with school by paying for my first few classes!

How and why do things like that happen? The whole deal defies conventional wisdom. Rick and I had known each other for maybe six to eight weeks when he suddenly got a prompting in his heart to offer financial support to help with my career. Just as easily as I had walked into his life, I could have walked out, check in hand, mouthing "Thanks a lot, sucker!" Sometimes the story unfolds that way. We hear about it on the news all the time. Ever heard of a guy named Bernie Madoff? Great guy, I'm sure, when you first met him.

The difference here was that GOD had brought Rick and me together. God had arranged the meeting. God had a bigger purpose in mind, a plan for the both of us. He knew that each of us was just what the other needed. God knew that our unique histories and individual sets of experiences—our virtues and our character flaws, our defeats and our pains, our victories, and our joys—would complement one another. Where we each had been, and where we were now, formed just the right combination to move His plan forward and to move us a couple of steps closer to becoming the men that He wanted us to be, that He knew we could be.

That's all God wants anyway—for us to cooperate with His plans rather than trying to forge our own. I know that for many people in the world, saying something like this is akin to saying that God wants us to be His little puppets, that we are just lifeless mannequins He manipulates to achieve His ends. But that couldn't be further from the truth. We have always had free will and the choice to do it our way at virtually every point in our lives. God's desire for us to cooperate with His plan for our lives is because He created each of us as unique beings; no two of us are completely alike, and as a loving creator, He wants the absolute best for His children, just as we do for ours.

During our early years, we may not have had genuine free will or control over our decisions. But that was not a condition that was forced upon us by God. That was the doing of our earthly parents, who hopefully had our best interests in mind. What kind of mother would just sit by and watch as their child tried to stick a screwdriver in an electrical socket? Or how about a father whose nine-year-old son asks to drive the family car? What kind of twisted logic and rationale would the father have to employ to let that happen?

History and personal experiences will certainly bear out the fact that many toddlers have gotten their hands on shiny knives, or daddy's gun, sometimes with devastating consequences. And we see stories in the media all the time about the child who somehow gets ahold of the keys and takes the family car for a little spin, sometimes with a tragic end. Except for some sick and evil individuals, parents who truly love their kids would do everything in their power to prevent these things from happening, wouldn't they? But as much as we love our children, we can't always fully protect them.

I believe God is just the same, with the exception being that He *can* prevent things from happening; it's just that He usually chooses not to. For just as we don't always jump in to stop our older children from making a questionable decision or foolish choice, God sometimes lets things play out. This is not because He derives pleasure from seeing His children struggling or in pain. It is so that we can learn valuable lessons like cause and effect and the fact that choices carry consequences.

God loves us too much to want to control us. He wants us to find our Rick when the time is right.

CHAPTER 18

ARE YOU READY TO LISTEN?

[11]"For I know the plans I have for you," declares the Lord, "plans to prosper you and not to harm you, plans to give you hope and a future. [12] Then you will call on me and come and pray to me, and I will listen to you. [13] You will seek me and find me when you seek me with all your heart." (JEREMIAH 29:11-13 NIV)

As I look over these stories, musings, and pontifications, it occurs to me that you, the reader, may have checked out long ago. And by "checked out," I don't mean that you stopped reading (Obviously, you are reading these words right now!). What I mean by checking out is that some of you who are still reading on but are sure that, while God may indeed talk to other people, He has never spoken to *you* and probably never will.

At the risk of beating a dead horse, I want to suggest once again that the issue is not God's silence. God is constantly speaking to us. The issue is that most of us are not open to the notion that maybe God has something to say to us personally. We know that there are billions of people in this world who are prettier, more intelligent, nicer, and more open-minded than we are. So, why would God want to reach out to us? Why would God take time out of His important day to send us a personal message? He has a great big universe to run, doesn't He? Powerful people don't have time for you and me, the average guy or gal.

Have you ever gotten a personal note from the president or CEO of your company saying that he or she was just thinking about you and wanted to encourage you during your time of trial? It wouldn't be practical for the CEO of a large corporation to take a deep and personal interest in each of the employees of their company. It is likely that they will never speak to or meet most of their employees anyway, so how would they even know that you were struggling with drug addiction? Or that your wife was ready to leave you, or that your Uncle Jim just found out he had Stage IV cancer? You can fill in the blanks with whatever you are struggling with! Unlike our hypothetical CEO, God sees it all—and He cares!

My experiences have brought me to a place where I know God is intimately interested in every detail of my life. Not just the big decisions or the life-or-death ones, but the mundane, everyday details. I believe this because, as a father of three beautiful children, I am interested in the small things that make up their lives—and I am an imperfect father. If this is how I yearn for my children as an imperfect father, how could God in all His perfection view His children with any less yearning? But more than as a loving Father, I see God as a trusted friend who is always available to listen to my struggles, to offer suggestions when appropriate, or maybe to just let me get something off my chest.

But it's not like I never get mad at God or question why He would let me go through something painful. I do get mad at God. I question why He does or doesn't do lots of things. Why didn't He intervene in the 2011 earthquake and devastating tsunami in Japan or the heartbreaking massacre at Sandy Hook? Why does He let horrors like child sex slavery not only persist but, by all reports, continue to grow? He could fix the problem of hunger simply by redistributing the resources of the world, but He doesn't. There are truly evil people who seemingly never get punished, and kind and generous people who never get rewarded. Why? Hopefully, you get the picture; the world is filled with injustices.

The question of how a loving God could allow terrible things to happen is not one I have a simple answer for, so I won't attempt to address it here. There are mountains of outstanding books that address the question of pain in the world. If this is a vexing problem for you, here are three books that I would encourage you to consider: *The Problem of Pain* by C.S. Lewis; and *The Gift of Pain* and *Where is God When It Hurts?* both by Philip Yancey.

The point I am trying to make is that God is interested in us and longs to spend time with us. Unlike even our closest friends and family members, He will keep pursuing us no matter how much grief we give Him. He will continue to pursue us even in our darkest and ugliest moments. In fact, that is precisely when He will woo us the hardest.

My sincerest hope and prayer is that after reading this, you will be open, even if just a little, to the notion that God speaks to you. With this new openness, I hope you will hear, and recognize, His voice speaking to you ... through the day-to-day interactions you have with other people; through your sorrows and your joys, your pain, and your healing; through the books you read and the stories you hear; through the roar of a tornado and the gentle whisper of the wind. If you can discern His voice, I hope you will start to understand and experience the incredible love that He has for you. With this newfound sense of hearing and awareness of God's love, you can let go of the notion that you control your life and be open to allowing God to direct it.

I can promise that if you give God control, you will be in for the ride of your life. God will take you to places you have never dreamed of—and I don't mean physical places like Bali or Bora Bora, although that is always a possibility. I'm talking about taking you to new spiritual depths, careers you never dreamed of, and places in your relationships that you never thought possible. I can also promise you that the journey will not be without pain and heartbreak; it will have both. But I can guarantee that if you are open to hearing God's voice, and if you are open to attributing to Him the promptings and thoughts that course through your daily life, then He will speak to you. He already does.

You may think right now, "How arrogant must one be to make these bold promises on God's behalf?" That would be an understandable reaction, but I would like to think that my promises come from a place of humility rather than arrogance. And I don't expect you to take my word for it. These are not my promises; they are God's promises. I'm just passing them along in my own imperfect but sincere way. My hope is that after reading these stories about how I have heard God in my life, you will start to hear Him in yours.

God is always speaking. Are you willing to listen?

"For God so loved the world that he gave his only begotten son, that whosoever believes in him should not perish but have everlasting life." (JOHN 3:16, NKJV)

ACKNOWLEDGEMENTS

How do I adequately thank all the people who have had an impact on my life that ultimately resulted in the writing of this book? I will come up short, but here goes!

First and foremost, I thank Lori, my wife of almost forty years, who has stuck with me through the victories and defeats; the good times and the hard times; the joys and the pains; and the laughter and the tears. I am the man I am today because of you!

Thank you to my incredible kids: Kellie, Thomas, and Erin who have put up with me and all my quirks over the years … I know I sometimes drove you crazy growing up. I am so proud to be your father!

Thank you to my parents, Tom and Judy who were always so supportive of me throughout my life … after I got through the terrible twos of course! Dad, I wish so much that you were still here with us. And Mom, you have always been my biggest cheer-leader. I'm not sure that I ever would have completed this project without you spurring me on.

To my siblings: Bessie, Michele, David, John, and Udee … we didn't always get along, and I was not always the best of role models, but we loved each other the best we could. I am blessed to call you my brothers and sisters.

Thank you to the many men I have come to know through the men's groups we have all belonged to over the years: Doug, Allen, Phil, Bobby, Scott, and Jeff you guys hold a special place in my heart. Thank you for allowing me to enter your lives, walk beside you, and grow together in our walk with Christ. And a thank you to my big brother Rick Kincaid ... Rick you never gave up on me!

To all of the pastors and leaders at *WestGate Church* in San Jose, who I have come to know over the years: Steve and Dana Clifford, Dave Larson, Ben Pierce, Scott and Debbie McDonald, Andy Gridley, Andy Barron, Mark and Lisa Averill, Keivan Tehrani, Jay Kim, and David Kim ... thank you for your teaching, rebuking, correcting and training in righteousness over the twenty plus years that I was there.

Thank you to my new church family at *A Jesus Church* in Oregon. I am just getting to know many of you but already you are having a huge impact on me!

Thank you to Steve Kuhn, who designed the cover and internals, Steven Miller who edited and guided me through to a final draft, and Aryn Van Dyke who helped market this first-time author's book!

But most importantly thank you to my loving Father in heaven, my risen savior Jesus Christ, and the Holy Spirit who dwells in me. Without your promptings, both sensational and mundane, this book would not have been written!

ABOUT THE AUTHOR

Mike McGeoy is a retired 'high-tech' professional who, at age 56, completed his MA in Marital & Family Therapy from Western Seminary. He interned at the Christian Counseling Center in San Jose and saw clients as an Associate MFT until moving to Portland with his wife in 2022. Born in Baltimore he spent his adolescent years in Israel and Chile before returning to the US for college. He was involved in many different church ministries over his 20+ years at WestGate Church in San Jose, but his heart is especially drawn to men's ministries and pre-marital counseling.